The Evolution of Economic Ideas and Systems

In order to fully understand the evolution and future growth of economic systems, we must draw on the lessons of economic history. The 2008 Financial Crisis, for example, mirrored past economic meltdowns with uncanny accuracy. Just like the Great Depression of the 1930s and the Savings and Loan Crisis of the 1980s, it featured deregulated lenders taking incredible risks with other people's money. Historical analysis is crucial to understanding trends and patterns that can help us predict the future.

This text presents a ground-breaking, pluralistic introduction to economic history and the history of economic thought. Tracing the development of economic systems and economic thought, the text introduces students to the story from ancient times to contemporary capitalism, and also its critics. Focusing in particular on Smith, Marx, Veblen, and Keynes, the text encourages students to consider which ideas and systems are still relevant in the modern world. This book can be used as a standalone text for relevant classes or as a supplement in any principles course.

Geoffrey Schneider is a Professor of Economics at Bucknell University, USA. He directs the International Confederation of Associations for Pluralism in Economics and he has published numerous books and articles from a pluralistic perspective.

The Evolution
of Economic Ideas
and Systems
A Pluralist Introduction

Geoffrey Schneider

Routledge
Taylor & Francis Group

LONDON AND NEW YORK

First published 2019
by Routledge
2 Park Square, Milton Park, Abingdon, Oxon OX14 4RN

and by Routledge
52 Vanderbilt Avenue, New York, NY 10017

Routledge is an imprint of the Taylor & Francis Group, an informa business

British Library Cataloguing-in-Publication Data
A catalogue record for this book is available from the British Library

Library of Congress Cataloging-in-Publication Data
Names: Schneider, Geoffrey Eugene, author.
Title: The evolution of economic ideas and systems:
a pluralist introduction/Geoffrey Schneider.
Description: Abingdon, Oxon; New York, NY: Routledge, 2019. |
Series: Routledge pluralist introductions to economics |
Includes bibliographical references and index.
Identifiers: LCCN 2018040207 (print) | LCCN 2018050738 (ebook) |
ISBN 9780429399367 (Ebook) | ISBN 9780367024758 |
ISBN 9780367024758 (hardback; alk. paper) |
ISBN 9780367024772 (pbk.; alk. paper) | ISBN 9780429399367(ebook)
Subjects: LCSH: Economics–History.
Classification: LCC HB75 (ebook) | LCC HB75 .S45423 2019 (print) |
DDC 330.09–dc23
LC record available at https://lccn.loc.gov/2018040207

ISBN: 978-0-367-02475-8 (hbk)
ISBN: 978-0-367-02477-2 (pbk)
ISBN: 978-0-429-39936-7 (ebk)

Typeset in Sabon and Helvetica
by Deanta Global Publishing Services, Chennai, India

Visit the series website: www.routledge.com/schneider

I dedicate this book to Charles Sackrey, Ph.D., my friend, co-author, co-conspirator, and inspiration for more than two decades. Charles was one of the best teachers and writers with whom I had the pleasure of working. He was the most open and honest teacher I ever observed. He was able to generate deep, meaningful, intellectual discussions with his students about complex and divisive issues. He stood up against injustice and supported every cause where people did the same. Thank you, Charles, for providing such a compelling vision of what a professor could be.

Contents

Figures

Preface

In 2008, the Financial Crisis confounded mainstream economists. Only a few of them predicted the meltdown was coming, and most were surprised and caught completely unprepared.

Interestingly, large numbers of political economists who were not part of the mainstream, including this author, anticipated the financial crisis and advised their friends and colleagues to pull their money out of financial markets prior to the collapse. What did political economists know that mainstream economists did not?

First, political economists drew on the lessons of economic history. There are numerous examples demonstrating that the deregulation of financial markets encourages speculative behavior, which can lead to spectacular booms and equally spectacular busts. The Great Depression of the 1930s, the Savings and Loan Crisis of the 1980s, and the Asian Financial Crisis of the 1990s all featured deregulated lenders taking incredible risks with other people's money. Similarly, the deregulation of financial markets in the 1980s and 1990s paved the way for the Great Financial Crises of 2008–2010, which sparked the Great Recession. Studying the evolution of economic systems and the regulatory environment can be particularly helpful in predicting when conditions are ripe for the next crisis.

Second, political economists drew on the economic ideas of Keynes, Marx, and Veblen, among others—economists who studied the roots of economic crises carefully and had much to say on the topic. Meanwhile, mainstream economists in the early 2000s were utilizing mathematical models that assumed markets would always be rational and efficient and could never experience a crisis. If your models assume that financial crises cannot occur, you certainly will not be able to see one coming! Thus, the analysis of the evolution of economic systems and a broader knowledge of economic ideas could have saved the mainstream economics profession from the embarrassment it suffered in 2008.

Even more surprising, perhaps, is the fact that most mainstream principles of economics texts *still* ignore economic history as well as some of the major economists whose ideas were most useful in predicting the financial crisis. This book seeks to remedy those omissions.

More specifically, most current principles of economics textbooks cover only mainstream economics, ignoring the rich ideas of heterodox schools of thought. They also tend to lack material on the great economists, so readers usually leave the introductory course without learning in depth about who Adam Smith, Karl Marx, Thorstein Veblen, Joseph Schumpeter, John Maynard Keynes, and Friedrich Hayek were and why their ideas are important.

Mainstream books are also missing the kind of historical analysis that is crucial to understanding trends and patterns that can help us predict certain aspects of the future. In addition, they tend to focus more on abstract models rather than on existing economic realities.

This book attempts to address some of these inadequacies. The book includes explicit coverage of the major heterodox schools of thought. This allows the reader to choose which ideas they find most compelling in explaining modern economic realities.

This book is intended to give you a broader background that will help save you from the tunnel vision that infected mainstream economics in recent decades. By understanding the evolution of economic systems and the ideas of the great economists, you will be better prepared to confront the complex realities of the modern world.

As you approach this material, it is important to keep an open mind. All of the major economists you will read about in this book were brilliant, and their ideas are worth studying. Each of them has devoted followers among modern economists. Your task is to consider all of these ideas and then, observing the world around you, decide which ideas make the most sense in understanding our modern economic system.

Acknowledgments

I would like to thank all of the research assistants who helped with the writing of this book. Those research assistants include Kailyn Angelo, Nghia (TN) Doan, James Elmendorf, Colin Randles, Kathryn Tomasi, Katelyn Schneider, and many others.

I would also like to thank my mentors who stimulated my interest in a broad-based, pluralistic approach to economics. In graduate school, William (Sandy) Darity and Vincent Tarascio taught pluralistically, embodying the values that I came to embrace. My colleagues at Bucknell University also provided a rich, engaging environment where our regular discussions of how to develop a pluralistic course and curriculum were invigorating. My regular collaborators on writing projects were particularly instrumental in developing a pluralistic approach, including Charles Sackrey, Janet Knoedler, Jean Shackelford, Berhanu Nega, Erdogan Bakir, and Steve Stamos.

My colleagues in various heterodox economics associations also were extremely importing in helping me to explore pluralistic ideas. In particular, members of the Association for Evolutionary Economics, the Union for Radical Political Economy, the Association for Social Economics, the Association for Institutional Thought, the International Association for Feminist Economics, and the International Confederation of Associations for Pluralism in Economics provided a rich intellectual environment in which to develop a pluralistic approach.

I am also deeply indebted to a number of economists whose ideas I draw on heavily in this book. In particular, Karl Polanyi's masterwork *The Great Transformation* looms large in the economic history material. Similarly, E. K. Hunt and Vincent Tarascio deeply influenced my work in the history of economic ideas.

I would also like to thank the staff at Routledge, and especially Editor Andy Humphries, who made this project possible. And, deep thanks are due to my family, Lori, Emily, and Kate, who put up with the many hours I spend at the computer writing.

PART I

Economics
A pluralistic definition

Part I explores several different definitions of what economics is and the different ways in which economists practice the social science of economics (economic methodology).

The first chapter, "What is economics?", begins by describing why economic policy matters to the country and to every person. It begins by describing the debate over whether or not politicians should balance their budgets every year given the regular occurrence of recessions in the economy (downturns in which unemployment increases and business activity decreases). The chapter then offers 4 different definitions of economics: One offered by mainstream economists (who tend to advocate a capitalist market system with limited government intervention), one preferred by economists practicing progressive political economy (PPE, which includes Institutionalist, Social, Post-Keynesian, and Feminist economists who believe capitalism can and should be reformed), another from economists who engage in radical political economy (RPE—Marxists and others who believe capitalism is fatally flawed and should be replaced), and a broad definition of pluralistic economics that synthesizes the other definitions.

Chapter 1 then takes up methodology, or how economists attempt to "do" economics. This will give you an idea of what it means to be an economist from the various perspectives—the kind of things you study, what you look for, and how you construct knowledge about the economy. The chapter then goes through a series of short examples so that you can see different types of economic analysis in action when economists study consumer behavior, labor markets, and the business cycle. The chapter concludes by briefly laying out the different schools of economics that will be discussed in the book.

Chapter 2, "Opportunity costs and production possibilities curves", takes up a simple mainstream economics concept, opportunity costs, and a simple economic model, the production possibilities curve (PPC). The PPC model is applied to several economic issues, including a treatment of defense spending and its impact on economic growth. The chapter concludes with a section on the potential limitations of economic models in capturing economic reality, building on the work of PPE and RPE economists.

What is economics?

The answer depends on who you ask

Each chapter in this book will begin with a list of learning goals. These goals will help you to focus on the key themes in the material.

1.0 CHAPTER 1 LEARNING GOALS

After reading this chapter you should be able to:

- Explain in your own words the importance of economics for you and for society as a whole;
- Briefly contrast unregulated market capitalism with mixed market capitalism;
- Describe the difference between mainstream economics, progressive political economy (PPE), and radical political economy (RPE), using their different definitions of economics and their different methods;
- Explain and begin to apply the methods of mainstream, PPE, and RPE economists to economic issues; and,
- Understand how the 10 different schools of economics match up with conservative, moderate, liberal, and radical political approaches to the economy.

Note that there is a lot of material in this chapter. However, the topics in this chapter will become clearer and clearer as the book progresses, so do not feel like you need to get all the details down now. Instead, work to grasp the basic ideas and gain a general understanding of the material.

1.1 WHY ECONOMICS MATTERS: ECONOMIC POLICY

Economics is a crucial subject that every educated voter and politician should understand. To show this, we begin with a brief example of how economic debates and a government's economic policy can matter to us all. As we go through this book, it is especially important for you to try to understand all of the different views of the various schools of economic thought that we will be studying. Understanding their differences teaches us more about this subject than any other way we might study it. As you read through this first example, and as a general rule while going through this book, take the time to try to figure out the meaning of each part of each section, including the key terms that are used, what they mean, and how they work.

Let's begin by taking a look at a government policy called *austerity*, **where governments reduce or eliminate social programs like food stamps, unemployment insurance, and education in order to balance the government budget** (they try to balance the incoming tax revenues with the spending amounts going out). Political leaders around the world regularly make the argument that the government should balance its budget each year, spending no more than it takes in via tax revenue. Such a policy is frequently justified by folksy expressions such as, "if households balance their checkbooks then the government should balance its budget." And this policy is sometimes supported by a few "crank" economists who are, in general, opposed to any type of government intervention. (These economists can be labelled "cranks" because their views have been dismissed by the vast majority of the economics profession.) The problem is that an obsession with balancing the government budget each and every year could cause an economic disaster. Here is a brief explanation for why it is a bad idea to try and balance the government budget when a recession hits.

In the modern U.S., the economy tends to hit a major crisis, called a recession, every 8–10 years. As you can see in Figure 1.1, the U.S. experienced recessions beginning in 1980, 1990, 2000 and 2008, when the U.S. real gross domestic product, which is the total output of goods and services, declined. A recession is usually sparked by a major panic of some sort, such as the financial crisis of 2007–2008 when stock markets plunged, banks failed, and the global economy shrank considerably. After a financial market collapse, businesses and consumers become pessimistic. Businesses lay off workers and consumers stop spending. This reduces overall spending in the economy, which reduces the incomes of both workers and business owners.

Reduced incomes in the economy mean that governments take in less tax revenue from income and sales taxes, and that the government will

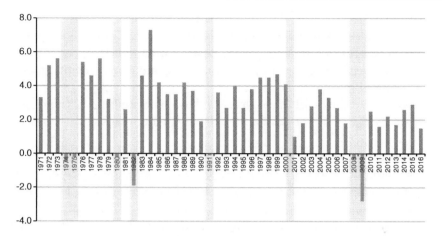

FIGURE 1.1 U.S. real gross domestic product (GDP) growth in the modern era (1971–2016).

start running a large budget deficit because tax revenues will have fallen below the level of government spending. How should the government respond to the fact that a recession caused a decline in incomes, which caused a decline in tax revenues and an increase in the government deficit? If the government decides to balance the government budget right away, then it must either raise taxes or cut spending, an economic policy called *austerity*. But, and here is where the crucial knowledge of economics comes in, *AUSTERITY WILL NOT SUCCEED IN BALANCING THE BUDGET IN A RECESSION!*

Here is why: If a nation's economy is in a recession, and if its government responds by raising taxes and cutting government spending, then the result will be that consumers and businesses have even *less* money to spend than before. Raising taxes directly reduces the money consumers and businesses have to spend. Reducing government spending directly reduces incomes: Teachers and other government personnel are laid off, construction firms see less revenue from building fewer roads and bridges, and so on. So cutting government spending and raising taxes directly reduces income and spending. Also, the decline in incomes and spending means additional reductions in tax revenues from income and sales taxes, making the government deficit *worse*! Thus, as any student of economics should know, trying to balance a government budget in a recession via austerity makes the recession worse, which makes the government deficit worse, not better.

Furthermore, even though it seems counterintuitive, governments can actually improve the deficit situation over the long term by spending more in a recession and running larger deficits! If the government cuts taxes and increases spending when a recession hits, which means running a larger budget deficit, it directly increases the incomes of consumers and the revenues of businesses. This leads consumers to spend more money and businesses to hire more people, raising incomes further, and increasing tax revenues in the process. By stimulating economic growth, government spending, and tax cuts can help to pay for themselves. (Before you go on, try reading back through the last two paragraphs until you understand the material. They contain a number of terms that we will deal with all semester.)

There are some major lessons to be learned from this example. First, what seems to be logical to most people (balancing one's budget every year) can fly in the face of what economists have learned. For example, the best way to combat a recession is for the government to increase spending, cut taxes, and inject money into the banking system to promote lending. Even though this will increase government deficits in the short term, it will likely stimulate economic growth, which will actually reduce deficits over the long term once economic growth is restored. However, efforts to balance the government budget in a recession via austerity will not work. When a recession hits, incomes and spending fall, and that reduces tax revenues, leading to substantial government deficits. If the government responds by raising taxes and cutting spending (austerity), this makes a fragile economy even worse, slowing economic growth, reducing incomes and tax revenues further, resulting in even more deficits.

Second, our example demonstrates that economics is an uncertain field, and there is much disagreement between economists from the different economic schools of thought. This means that it is usually possible for politicians to find support for their ideas, no matter how bad those ideas are. Politicians frequently seize on bad ideas from crank economists because those ideas support their political perspective, even though most of the economics profession would consider those ideas to be ridiculous. This was certainly true of austerity policies, which have been promoted recently by a few crank economists but opposed by most economists.

Your job, as you read through this book, is to understand and evaluate the best ideas that economists have about how the economy works and what economic policies should be used in certain situations. However, we need to avoid making the mistake that some politicians do when they listen only to the economists who say what they want to hear. Instead, critically evaluate the ideas of all the economists you study, assess the available evidence, and develop your own perspective regarding which economic ideas best explain the world you see around you. The world is desperately in need of economically literate people who will call politicians on their craziest economic ideas. You will find that a solid understanding of the economy will help you in your personal life as well.

1.2 HOW DOES THE ECONOMY AFFECT YOUR LIFE?

The economy is vitally important to each of us. Consider for a minute the following factors that affect what your life and your community are like:

- An austerity program could slash government funding for financial aid and other programs at your college, resulting in huge increases in tuition and layoffs (possibly of a family member);
- The economic system largely determines if you get enough food to eat, the various kinds of opportunities for work that are available to you, what your workday is like, and whether or not our society is equal or unequal
- Major economic events, such as financial crises, economic booms, and shifts in major industries, can have a huge influence on your life and your community;
- The functioning of the global economy determines what the planet is like, including how much pollution there is and if beautiful coastlines are owned by particular people or if they are public parks;
- In the modern economy, businesses produce an ever-changing, ever-expanding quantity of goods and services for sale to people, often using extensive advertising to increase sales;
- Large corporations play a particularly important role in today's global economy, determining what goods are sold, where they are produced, and what future endeavors they think are worth investing in;
- Governments play a major role in establishing the rules of the economic system, shaping what types of economic activities are undertaken— often regulating the behaviors of companies and individuals—and sometimes developing or promoting key industrial sectors;
- Global trade has a significant impact on jobs and communities, promoting growth in some places while undermining it in others.

To study such important topics, the social science of economics developed. Economists seek to understand the above factors and many more. If they can successfully determine how the economy works, economists can then make useful recommendations regarding how the economy can be improved.

The study of the economy can be quite difficult, however. The world economy is extremely complex, involving almost 200 countries, more than 7 billion people from culturally diverse backgrounds, and millions of organizations interacting in a variety of situations. Economists are often able to recognize trends and patterns, which can allow us to make accurate predictions. Yet, as is commonly known, economists are frequently wrong in their predictions due to the complex nature of the economy. In other words, economics is an inexact social science. Furthermore, the fact that the study of the economy is uncertain and inexact means that at any given time economists will often disagree with each other over what is happening in the economy and what should be done in order to improve its outcomes.

Economists also disagree over what type of economy we should have. As we will see below, some advocate an economy based on unregulated markets in which private individuals and corporations make most of the economic decisions without the interference of government (unregulated market capitalism). Others tend to see markets as bad for people and the environment, preferring to have workers and a democratically elected government in control of the major economic decisions (democratic socialism). Most economists advocate a middle path between these two perspectives: Mixed market capitalism.

1.3 WHY TAKE A PLURALISTIC APPROACH TO THE STUDY OF ECONOMICS?

Because there are debates and divisions among economists regarding the nature of the economy and the role of public policy in it, this book takes a *pluralistic* approach. Pluralistic economics seeks to include the best ideas from all major economic perspectives, while also highlighting the important areas of agreement and disagreement. This book will share the best ideas from a wide variety of economists, and you are tasked with the job of deciding which ideas are most relevant to the world you see around you. For instance, do you think markets are usually efficient and effective, as Adam Smith believed, or do they tend to be ruthless and exploitative as Karl Marx argued? Is government intervention in markets inherently inefficient, as Friedrich Hayek believed, or is government intervention essential to the healthy functioning of markets, as John Maynard Keynes maintained?

One clear way to differentiate between some of the different schools of thought is to consider their definitions of the study of economics.

Mainstream economics (ME) is **the study of how society manages its scarce resources to satisfy individuals' unlimited wants.** To mainstream economists, economics involves studying the costs and benefits of the decisions facing consumers, producers and governments, and making rational choices between alternatives using society's limited resources. Mainstream economists are particularly good at establishing the consistent statistical relationships between economic variables. These ideas can be used to predict, for example, how an increase in the price of gasoline is likely to affect the demand for gasoline, or how an increase in consumer spending will affect a country's total income and its unemployment rate and inflation rate. Mainstream economics includes both conservative economists who prefer little government intervention in markets and liberal economists who see government intervention in markets as essential.

Progressive political economics (PPE) is the study of social provisioning—the economic processes that provide the goods and services required by society to meet the needs of its members. These economists study culture, history, and technology to understand how the economy is evolving over time, and how different societies function in distinct ways. Progressive political economists are particularly good at analyzing matters such as how consumers in Germany behave differently than consumers in the US, or how the legal and political systems in a particular country affect their economic system.

Radical political economics (RPE) is the study of power relations in society, especially conflicts over the allocation of a society's resources by various social classes, and how those conflicts cause society to evolve. Radical political economists see power, conflict, and technology as the major drivers of changes in economic systems. They are particularly good at analyzing how class relations affect the economic system and the dynamics of how economic crises form.

If we combine definitions, a pluralistic definition of economics would be as follows: *Pluralistic economics* is a social science whose practitioners, from a variety of distinct schools of thought, study economies, how they grow and change, and how they produce and distribute the goods that societies need and want.

Another important topic is the different ways to study the economy. Next, we turn to the different *methods* that economists use in economics.

1.4 ECONOMIC METHODOLOGY: HOW TO "DO" ECONOMICS

Given the vast complexity of the global economy, it is impossible for economists to study everything. Thus, they choose to narrow their focus on the variables that they see as most important.

Mainstream economists attempt to be as scientific as possible. The mainstream economics methodology can be summarized as follows:

1. **Mainstream economists make simplifying assumptions about the economy so that they can focus on what they determine to be the most important economic variables.**

For example, mainstream economists typically believe that consumers are rational, calculating, fully informed, and self-interested most of the time. In theory, this allows mainstream economists to assume all consumers behave in a consistent manner, which should allow mainstream economists to make reasonable predictions about consumers' economic behavior. Thus, mainstream economic models are based on a hypothetical "**economic man**" who behaves quite predictably.

2. **Mainstream economists construct mathematical models of the economy so that they can make predictions about how it will behave.**

   Mainstream economists make logical deductions based on their assumptions and construct hypothesis about how the economy should work if their assumptions hold. For example, if we assume consumers are rational, well-informed, and self-interested, then we can construct a model of consumer demand demonstrating that when the price of a product increases, consumers will buy less of that good for themselves. This is known as the law of demand, and it can be expressed as a mathematical equation or as a graph, such as Figure 1.2.

3. **Mainstream economists test their models using statistical analysis and observations of whether or not the real world conforms to their predictions.**

   If the assumptions are reasonably accurate and the models are good, then the predictions of mainstream economic models should match what we see in the real world. For example, historically, a 10 percent increase in the price of gasoline caused a 2 percent decrease in the quantity of gasoline purchased by consumers. Thus, assuming no changes in the assumptions behind the model, and holding all other economic variables constant, we could predict that a gasoline tax that raised the price of gasoline by 100 percent would cause consumers to purchase 20 percent less gasoline than usual.

Political economists—those from the PPE and RPE groups—believe that the methods adopted by mainstream economists are fundamentally flawed, and thus approach the study of economics quite differently. Indeed, they see each of the assumptions behind "economic man" as flawed in key ways. From the political economy perspective, consumers can be irrational and ill-informed much of the time. And whereas a fully-informed, calculating and rational individual would never be convinced to buy something he or she doesn't need, we know that most of us are affected by advertising in key ways, such as making impulsive purchases or buying products we do not really need at prices that we know are too high for our budgets.

More interesting and more important, from the political economy perspective, are the social factors that shape consumers and their decisions. How does culture (peer pressure, social groups, etc.) shape consumers' tastes and purchases? How do companies manipulate consumers via advertising

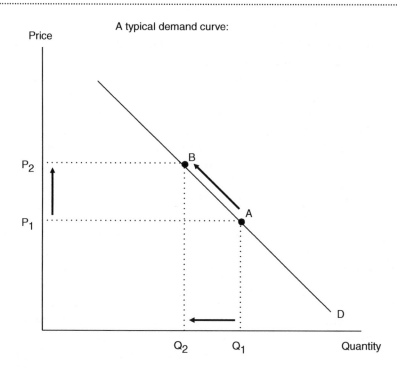

FIGURE 1.2 A typical demand curve.

and attempting to control the market? How does one's gender, race, and social class affect one's purchases? Is it truly rational to buy consumer goods that are not necessary for survival when those goods use resources that contribute to global warming? Or is such consumerist behavior the unique product of a particular culture in a particular place at a specific time?

In order to differentiate between the two approaches to economics highlighted above, the next section uses the ideas of both mainstream and political economists to analyze consumer shopping behavior on Amazon.com. Notice that *both* perspectives contribute something valuable to our understanding of consumer behavior, which is why a pluralistic approach to economics is likely to leave you with a better understanding of the economy!

1.5 METHODOLOGY IN MICROECONOMICS: AMAZON.COM AND CONSUMER BEHAVIOR

Economics is traditionally broken up into the study of microeconomics and macroeconomics. Microeconomics is the study of how individual markets work, such as the market for labor, cell phones, or other specific goods and services. Macroeconomics is the study of the dynamics of national and international economies, including the factors affecting recessions and booms, economic growth, and financial markets.

To explore microeconomic analysis from a mainstream and a political economy (PPE/RPE) perspective, we turn to an analysis of the shopping behavior of consumers with the online retailing giant Amazon. com. Amazon.com is world's largest online retailer, and it analyzes consumer behavior relentlessly in the pursuit of higher sales. Thus, we learn a lot about consumers from the various strategies that Amazon.com uses successfully.

To improve sales, mainstream economists would emphasize the importance of providing rational, calculating, fully informed, and self-interested consumers with the best product at the best price. This is, indeed, one of Amazon.com's signature strengths. For books, music, and electronics, Amazon.com is consistently cheaper than its competitors. For other goods, such as groceries or household appliances, Amazon.com tends to be slightly more expensive than Wal-Mart or local grocery stores. However, many consumers continue to shop for these goods at Amazon.com for the convenience (consumers' time is also a "cost"). Amazon.com provides a lot of information for consumers about their products, including customer reviews so that consumers can make an informed decision. Thus, much consumer behavior on Amazon.com confirms the mainstream view.

However, PPE and RPE economists look at additional factors. First, consumers on Amazon.com are often impulsive. This is why Amazon.com often gives you suggestions when you shop, telling you what other consumers bought who purchased the same items you did, and giving you personalized recommendations. As we know, for many consumers, the suggestions have a significant impact on their buying behavior. Thus, from a PPE or RPE perspective, we must also study consumers' impulsive side, especially the ways that sellers work on us, even to the point of hiring psychologists to study how best we can be tricked and fooled.

Second, consumers are affected by culture, and especially the behavior of their peers. This is one of the reasons why customer reviews are so successful. People feel much more secure in making a purchase if their peers approve of the item. For this and many other reasons, PPE and RPE economists view culture as an essential subject of study.

Third, Amazon.com exercises its market power to compete unfairly. The company demands that publishers discount books and other sellers discount items that are provided to Amazon.com, or it will refuse to offer those entities' items for sale. This is a strategy also pursued by Wal-Mart. By demanding and getting lower prices from their suppliers, the big retailers get a cost advantage over smaller competitors, allowing them to sell goods for lower prices and to reap higher profits because they are bigger and more powerful, not because they provide better goods or services. Analyzing the main institutions in a society, and the power and control exercised by those institutions, is another important topic to PPE and RPE economists, and surely among the most important differences between the methodology of political economists and that of mainstream economists.

Fourth, some retailers whose products are sold on Amazon.com try to cheat the system by paying people to review their products favorably. Consumers who are taken in by these reviews will not be purchasing an item based on valid information. Understanding a country's legal system, and how the profit motive can lead to unsavory behavior, is another topic of focus for PPE and RPE economists.

What we can see is that mainstream economics focuses on certain aspects of consumer behavior while PPE and RPE economists broaden that focus considerably. We see similar divisions in the area of macroeconomics, as will be found below. But first, it is worth considering the scientific approach to economics more carefully.

1.6 THE SCIENTIFIC METHOD IN ECONOMICS: HOW SCIENTIFIC CAN ECONOMICS BE?

The scientific approach to economics, in which economists make simplifying assumptions to construct models and then test those models against the real world, is often called positive economics. This is named after the economic philosophy of positivism, which seeks to determine definitive, "positive" facts about how the economy works, without the influence of political biases. This approach has yielded some very useful information about the economy, but there are limits to how scientific economics can be.

For example, for many years economists using a model of the labor market believed that there was an inverse relationship between wages and employment: It seemed logical that if wages were increased, businesses would hire fewer workers due to the increase in costs (assuming there were no other major changes in the economy happening at the time that might alter that basic relationship). However, in a groundbreaking study in the 1990s, economists David Card and Alan Krueger proved that a higher minimum wage had no effect on employment; businesses needed a certain minimum number of employees to serve their customers and did not lay off workers after the minimum wage went up. Following the work of Card and Krueger, many other studies of the minimum wage were undertaken, with most supporting their work (some contradicted the findings, though). Overall, the studies seem to indicate that raising the minimum wage by a modest amount usually has little or no effect on employment, although sometimes a higher minimum wage may reduce employment very slightly.

We learn several important things from this example. First, scientific economics can be extremely useful if it can successfully determine how the economy works, which can then inform governments of the best economic policies to use. Second, it is very difficult to establish "positive" and conclusive economic facts. Due to the conflicting findings of numerous studies, economists still disagree on whether or not we should raise the minimum wage. Third, the uncertain nature of the "science" of economics means that economists usually disagree about the way the world works and what policies should be adopted. There are limits to how scientific the study of economics can be. Fourth, logical analysis, while useful, can have serious pitfalls. The logic of the model of the labor market implies that any increase in the wage rate will lead to a decrease in employment, but real-world data indicates that this logic seems to be flawed much of the time.

We see similar disagreements in macroeconomics, especially in the study of economic crises.

1.7 MACROECONOMIC ANALYSIS OF ECONOMIC CRISES

One of the most striking differences between mainstream economics and political economics became apparent in the lead up to the Financial Crisis of 2007–2008. Prior to the crisis, most mainstream economists held the view that the macroeconomy tended to be stable. They believed the macroeconomy tended to reach a stable equilibrium from which there would only be small, unimportant deviations. Mainstream economists, using sophisticated mathematical and statistical techniques, were able to develop elaborate general equilibrium models to analyze the interaction between key macroeconomic variables. These models helped the Federal Reserve Bank of the U.S. and other national banks tweak interest rates in order to keep economies growing and relatively stable. These models, however, did not account for the possibility of an economic crisis occurring.

Meanwhile, political economists, especially those who study economic crises and how they form, began to be concerned with the housing bubble forming in the U.S. that was causing an the exceptionally rapid increase in the value of financial assets associated with housing markets. To political economists, economic crises are frequent occurrences, due to the fundamental instability in businesses' investment decisions and the potential for a shortfall in consumer and investor spending once confidence is eroded by some sort of economic shock.

From the political economy perspective, economies typically follow a business cycle of about 10 years in length. After a recession starts, businesses are very pessimistic and investment spending on factories and equipment declines. Households are pessimistic and millions of people have lost jobs, so consumer spending also declines. After a few years of sluggish growth, the economy usually starts to pick up. Businesses need to replace outdated and worn out equipment, and new, profitable opportunities emerge, so business investment rises. This puts more people to work, improving consumer confidence, and consumer spending also increases, raising businesses' profits. This, in turn, stimulates more business investment and hiring. The economy begins to boom and businesses' profits grow rapidly. Businesses have substantial profits, and they invest heavily to take advantage of new opportunities. But eventually, after the economy has boomed for several years, the most secure business opportunities are already taken, and businesses invest their profits in increasingly risky ventures. Eventually, these risky ventures crash and the economy falls into another recession.

For example, in the early 2000s, businesses in the US invested in extremely risky financial securities tied to real estate markets, which tend to be quite volatile. The value of these risky securities increased incredibly rapidly as more and more money poured in. But eventually investors realized that the real estate market was over-valued, and they sold the risky securities in a panic. The result was a crash in the financial markets, which eliminated billions of dollars in investor wealth, undermined consumer confidence, and threw the economy into the Great Recession of 2008. Prior to the Great Recession, a number of political economists (and 1 mainstream economist!) published material predicting the financial crisis, and a number of political economists (including the author of this book) quietly began advising their friends that a crisis was coming.

In the wake of the Great Recession, most mainstream economists returned to the work of the great economist John Maynard Keynes, whose analysis of recessions formed the basis of the ideas political economists used to anticipate the recession. There is now more similarity between mainstream economics and political economics in macroeconomics, although mainstream economists still see the macroeconomy as fundamentally stable whereas political economists see it as volatile and unstable. It would be wise for an economics student to understand both views! This is a topic we will take up at length in later chapters.

1.8 THE RICH SOCIAL SCIENCE OF ECONOMICS

Previous sections of this chapter explored microeconomic and macroeconomic examples of how different economists view important economic issues. You should now have some idea of the richness of the field of economics and the insights you can gain from some of the schools of thought. Each school of thought has crucial ideas that you will find useful in understanding certain aspects of the economy you see around you.

Note that, at times, we will broaden our definition of economics to cover 10 different schools of economic thought. Each of these schools of thought uses a particular method of analysis and has areas in which their analysis is particularly insightful. Those schools of thought are listed in Figure 1.3.

There is often much overlap between various groups, so do not view the schools of thought as rigid. Conservative mainstream economists, including Monetarist, New Classical, and Supply Side economists, share

Economic School of Thought	Methodology	Key Areas of Strength	Some major thinker(s)
Austrian	Focus on individual choices and their impact on the economy; tend to avoid the use of models and statistics and the analysis of group behavior	Efficiency of markets, and how public policy can be stifling, corrupted and inefficient	Friedrich Hayek, Ludwig von Mises
Monetarist	Mainstream Economics: Make simplifying assumptions about economic actors, construct economic models to make predictions, and (to the extent possible) test those predictions using statistical analysis	Importance of the money supply in affecting inflation, Gross Domestic Product	Milton Friedman
New Classical (Rational Expectations)		How individuals' rational decisions can anticipate market changes and affect the economy	Robert Lucas, Eugene Fama
Supply Side		How tax rates and regulations affect individuals and businesses, and economic activity in general	Martin Feldstein
Moderate (New Keynesian)		Markets are effective, but they need appropriate regulation to fix market failures and operate more efficiently.	Paul Krugman, Joseph Stiglitz
Institutional	Focus on the evolution of key human institutions and group behaviors, including technology and culture	How an economy is fundamentally shaped by its institutions, including culture, social norms, companies, the legal system and government	Thorstein Veblen, John Kenneth Galbraith
Social	Focus on the ethics and social impact of economic activities and policies, along with social (as well as self-interested) behavior	The ethical and social causes and consequences of economic behavior, institutions, organizations, theory, and policy	E. K. Hunt, John B. Davis
Feminist	Attempt to overcome male, patriarchal biases by analyzing social constructs, discrimination and inequities	Economics of households, and the impact of gender on economic outcomes	Marilyn Waring, Nancy Folbre
Post-Keynesian	Focus on effective demand (spending), investment instability and money creation of banks as major economic factors	How demand affects the macroeconomy, and how instability and uncertainty affect investment	Hyman Minksy, Paul Davidson
Marxist	Focus on class conflict over the wealth (surplus product) produced by workers, and the dynamics produced by this conflict	Exploitative and unstable nature of markets, and the effect of capitalism on workers and communities	Karl Marx, Friedrich Engels

FIGURE 1.3 Methodology and strengths of 10 major economic schools of thought.

much with Austrian economists, preferring a mostly unregulated capitalist market system in which private firms own and control the major economic resources of society, and allocate those resources based on the activities that earn the most profit. Moderate mainstream economists (also known as New Keynesians) believe that markets must be carefully regulated by the government in order to reduce the negative side of markets, such as economic crises, pollution, and inequality. Progressive political economists, including Institutional, Social, Feminist, and Post-Keynesian economists, along with the most liberal mainstream economists, want the government to play a larger role in society, managing and guiding markets rather than letting markets dictate the direction of the economy. Finally, radical political economists, drawing on the ideas of Karl Marx, see markets as ruthless and exploitative, and they would rather replace capitalist markets with some variety of socialism or communism.

The 10 schools of economic thought are laid out in Figure 1.4, based on how much or how little government the economists from each school tend to prefer, which is perhaps the central issue that creates the different approaches to each school of thought.

Fortunately, there is enough overlap between various schools of thought that we will often simplify our discussion to a few major perspectives on key topics. With respect to policy issues, it is often possible to break economists down into conservative, liberal, and radical groups.

Conservative economists generally favor unregulated market capitalism with less government intervention. *Unregulated market capitalism* is an economic system in which the main productive resources of society— the labor, land, machinery, equipment, and natural resources—are owned by private individuals who use those resources to produce goods and services that are bought and sold in markets for profit.

Liberal (and moderate) economists believe in regulated or "mixed" market capitalism. *Mixed market capitalism* is an economic system in

More Markets, Less Government						Less Markets, More Government
Economic School of Thought		Mainstream			PPE	RPE	Economic School of Thought
	Austrian	Monetarist, New Classical	Supply Side	Moderate (New Keynesian)	Institutional, Social, Feminist, Post-Keynesian	Marxist	
Preferred economic system	Unregulated Market Capitalism	Unregulated Market Capitalism	Pro-Business Capitalism	Regulated Market Capitalism	Managed Market Capitalism	Socialism, Communism	Preferred economic system
Political views	Conservative			Moderate	Liberal	Socialist	Political views

FIGURE 1.4 Different kinds of economics.

which private sector firms and individuals produce goods and services for markets for profit, and a public sector established by the government regulates those markets and provides public goods such as schools, roads, airports, health care, and other goods and services that are usually provided inadequately by private markets. Most of the economies in the world have chosen this type of economic system because it has the benefits of a market system, including innovations, competition, and economic growth, without the worst problems you tend to see in unregulated market capitalism, such as exploitation of workers or the environment.

Radical economists are highly suspicious of markets, seeing them as dominated by a handful of wealthy corporations and rich individuals. They prefer *democratic socialism*, an economic system in which the most important resources of society are controlled democratically by all citizens, including workers who usually have little say in how market capitalist economies are run. From this perspective, markets are not particularly efficient, as they produce wasteful and unnecessary goods while neglecting other, more important things such as public health, leisure time with one's family, workers' quality of life, and the environment.

Depending on which economists have the most influence and the economic views of politicians, the economic systems of countries around the globe exhibit substantial variations. Almost all modern economies can be classified as mixed market capitalist, in that they depend on markets for the production and distribution of most goods and services, but they also utilize a substantial degree of government intervention.

As you can see from Figure 1.5, which depicts the size of the government sector in selected economies around the world, the U.S. has the smallest government of any developed economy, coming the closest to unregulated market capitalism. One of the reasons for this is that the U.S. is the only developed economy without a national health care system. Even very market-oriented countries like the United Kingdom (U.K.) and Australia provide national health care to all citizens. Economies such as Sweden's and Norway's, while still predominantly market-based, come closer to democratic socialism in that they have very large state sectors that provide important goods and services such as college education, child care, dental care, and housing for any citizen who needs them.

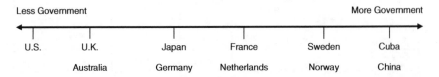

FIGURE 1.5 The size of government in select economies.

As communist countries, Cuba and China have the most government intervention. ***Communism* is an economic system in which the government controls society's productive resources and makes the major economic decisions.** However, both Cuba and China utilize markets to some degree, so even their economies are "mixed."

1.9 CONCLUSION

This chapter described why economics is an important subject to study. It also detailed various definitions of what economics is. The differences between mainstream economics and political economics (PPE and RPE) were covered, along with how the conservative, liberal, and radical political approaches to economics affect the size of government in various economies. Remember that each school of economic thought has something useful to add to our understanding of the economy, so it is important to study each approach. In the areas where economic approaches disagree, your job is to critically analyze the different perspectives and to decide for yourself which ideas best capture the world you see around you. This should leave you with a sophisticated and useful understanding of the world.

Also, the economic views that a society chooses to adopt determine the type of economic system that a society develops. Conservative economic views result in an economy closer to unregulated market capitalism. Moderate economic views result in a mixed market capitalist economic system that is mostly market-oriented but which includes government intervention to fix the worst problems in markets. If liberal economic views are adopted, the result is a mixed market capitalist economic system with a larger role for government in directing and guiding markets. Finally, a radical economic view would result in a democratic socialist or communist economic system, in which the role of markets is very small and where most economic decisions are made by citizens or by the government.

To clarify the different types of economics, Chapter 2 goes through a mainstream economic model, the production possibilities curve, and contrasts this approach with the views of political economists.

QUESTIONS FOR REVIEW

1. What is **austerity**? Why do most economists think it is a bad economic policy to pursue in a recession?

2. Read about what is happening in the nation or around the globe in a reputable magazine or newspaper, such as the *New York Times, Wall Street Journal, The Economist, The Financial Times,* or *The Guardian.* Which events would be considered relevant to the study of *economics,* given the definitions of economics in this chapter? How are these events important to people and their communities? Explain briefly.

3. What are the primary differences between mainstream economics and political economics (PPE and RPE)? Explain briefly in your own words.

4. Consider the description of "economic man" above, and the description of positive, scientific economics. Also consider how political economists (PPE and RPE) study human behavior. Then reflect carefully on your own shopping habits. Do you usually make rational, calculated, fully informed purchases (like "economic man"), or do you tend to buy on impulse for a variety of reasons, or do you do both? Analyze how much of your purchasing behavior can be captured by "positive economics," and when the methods used by political economists would better reflect your behavior. How much of your shopping behavior could be predicted scientifically? How much of it would be hard to predict?

5. Briefly explain the main differences between the economic systems of unregulated market capitalism, mixed market capitalism, and democratic socialism. Using a recent issue of *The Economist* or another reputable publication that features significant international economic news, find examples that show how two countries exhibit characteristics of one or more of these types of economic systems.

6. One of the main economic problems in the modern world is climate change. Scientists have concluded that the world is likely to experience a major ecological crisis unless we reduce the amount of greenhouse gases (especially carbon) that we produce. Greenhouse gases are generated by economic activity. Almost all economists acknowledge the problem but disagree vehemently on how to solve it. Given the definitions of radical, moderate, and conservative economists in the reading, identify which group would be most likely to support each set of policies listed below. Explain your answer briefly.

   a. Establish a carbon tax (on fossil fuels) to give businesses and consumers incentives to change their behavior.

   b. Subsidize the development of solar and wind power industries while taxing carbon to push the economy toward more sustainable practices.

c. Close down the most harmful industries (coal, shale gas), tax carbon and mandate the comprehensive use of renewable energies in the very near future; create jobs for any displaced workers.

7. Which of the 10 schools of economic thought listed in Figure 1.3 do you find most interesting? Which do you find least interesting? What does this indicate about your own background and approach to economics at this point?

Scarcity, choice, and opportunity cost

The mainstream approach, the PPC model, the limits of this approach, and the importance of institutions

In this chapter we will examine some mainstream economic concepts, including scarcity, opportunity cost, efficiency, cost benefit analysis, and how those concepts frame the choices faced by a society. We will also use a simple mainstream economic model, the production possibilities curve (PPC), to capture some of these concepts and to display a variety of choices that a society might face. We will apply these concepts and the PPC model to several economic issues, including an analysis of defense spending and its impact on economic growth. The chapter concludes by drawing on the work of political economists to show the limitations of these mainstream economic concepts and the PPC model in capturing economic reality. Rather than focusing on scarcity and choice, political economists tend to focus on the institutions that shape a society and its choices.

2.0 CHAPTER 2 LEARNING GOALS

After reading this chapter you should be able to:

- Define and apply the concepts of scarcity, opportunity cost, efficiency, and cost benefit analysis;
- Use a production possibilities curve to analyze the opportunity cost of allocating resources in a particular way;

- Identify and explain the difference between capital goods and consumer goods, and analyze their impact on economic growth using a PPC;
- Explain why political economists find the mainstream approach to scarcity and cost benefit analysis limited, and how political economists would approach these topics differently using an analysis of the institutional factors that shape a society's choices; and,
- Critically analyze the strengths and limitations of the production possibilities curve model and the political economy approach to choices regarding the allocation of resources.

Work on understanding each new concept in this chapter carefully. Also, spend some time working with the production possibilities curve to make sure you understand how it works and what it can be used for. Finally, the chapter is primarily concerned with how mainstream economists and political economists study the choices a society makes to allocate its resources. As always, critically analyze the different approaches, and develop your own ideas on the topic.

2.1 SCARCITY, CHOICE, AND OPPORTUNITY COST

The problem of scarcity is absolutely central to mainstream and Austrian economics (this is one of several areas in which mainstream economics and Austrian economics overlap). *Scarcity* exists **when a society's seemingly unlimited desire for goods and services exceeds the resources available to produce and provide those goods and services.** From this perspective, scarcity exists everywhere because there are never enough resources to produce everything society wants, and much of human life is a struggle to overcome scarcity. Consumers always want more than they have—bigger houses, better cars, faster smart phones, trendier clothes, more new stuff of all kinds—but they have limited budgets. Companies want to produce more goods so they can generate higher profits, but they have limited inputs (labor, machinery, technology, buildings, raw materials). Governments would like to build more roads, improve the environment, spend more on social programs and expand their militaries, but they have limited tax revenues to spend. Thus, society as a whole wants more of everything it values. However, because of limited resources, people cannot have everything they want, which necessitates making difficult choices. *Choice* involves **consumers, producers, and governments selecting from among the limited options that are available to them due to scarcity.**

Mainstream economists like to frame making choices in terms of cost-benefit analysis: Good decisions depend on carefully weighing the costs and benefits involved in a decision. In order to undertake such analysis, economists use the concept of *opportunity cost*: **What is given up when a choice is made to allocate resources in a particular way.** When a consumer is considering the purchase a $40,000 car, what is the **next best alternative** for which they could use that money? They could put an addition on their home, work 2000 fewer hours at their job, buy 4000 cases of cheap beer, among many other things. A rational decision would weigh the benefits of the new car against the value of what is perceived as the next best alternative to that car, which would be considered the car's opportunity cost.

The concept of opportunity cost can be a powerful tool in improving decision-making because it forces us to consider not just the benefit of what we are choosing to devote resources to, but all alternative uses of those resources as well. Consider the following examples.

The opportunity cost of attending college

The average cost of four years of tuition and room and board in 2014–2015 was $76,000 at a public university and $131,000 at a private university in the U.S. But one must consider more than just the financial cost. Instead of going to college, a person with a high school degree could go to work full-time and earn, on average, $30,000 per year. So the financial opportunity cost of attending college for 4 years is about $196,000 at a public university, including $120,000 in foregone salary and $76,000 in tuition and room and board. Similarly, the opportunity cost of attending a private college would be $251,000, on average. Is this a good investment? Fortunately for college students, the lifetime earnings of a typical U.S. college graduate—about $1,200,000—are more than double the $580,000 that a typical high school graduate would earn in their lifetime, so a college education clearly has a substantial financial benefit. Also, college education provides opportunities to cultivate one's passions, become an informed voter, learn to work with diverse people, and much, much more.

The opportunity cost of Sony devoting resources to its computer division

The Japanese company Sony once had a very large computer division. However, personal computer sales began to drop while mobile device (smart phones and tablets) sales surged after 2010, so Sony decided to sell off its computer division. Given the poor prospects for personal computers, it made little sense to continue to devote so many resources to that area. For Sony, the opportunity cost of running its computer division was the resources and staff that it could instead devote to the rapidly growing market for mobile devices.

The opportunity cost of the U.S. government spending $55 billion on B-2 Stealth Bombers

The stealth bomber was designed during the Cold War to evade Soviet radar systems and empower the U.S. to drop nuclear bombs on them. The Soviet Union collapsed in 1990, and most modern conflicts utilize drones much more than old fashioned bombers. Nonetheless, the U.S. Air Force recently asked for $55 billion for a fleet of new B-2 bombers. What is the opportunity cost of this purchase? In other words, what else could the government do with $55 billion? They could provide 723,684 people with a free education at a public university. They could give every taxpayer a $450 tax cut. These are just two of many worthwhile options.

As you can see from the above examples, the concept of opportunity cost can be applied to almost any decision facing consumers, companies or governments. An analysis of opportunity cost can help people make a carefully considered choice between two viable alternatives.

Note that the idea of opportunity cost only makes sense if resources are being used efficiently. *Efficiency* in mainstream economics refers to a situation in which **all resources are employed as productively as possible.** No resources are being wasted or used inefficiently. Efficiency matters because if there are unused resources or if resources are being used inefficiently, then more goods can be produced by putting all resources into use or by using resources more efficiently. There is *no opportunity cost* when production in increased by employing unused or inefficiently used resources. Nothing has to be given up.

For example, if everyone in a country is employed, then producing more of one good necessarily means producing less of other goods. Producing more bombers for national defense means producing fewer cars for consumers. However, the average U.S. unemployment rate from 2005–2015 was 6.8 percent. If all the unemployed were put to work, a huge amount of additional goods and services could be provided for no opportunity cost (without sacrificing the production of any other good or service).

Mainstream economists have developed a simple economic model to display the choices that societies, especially individuals, companies, and governments face when allocating scarce resources: The production possibilities curve.

2.2 THE PRODUCTION POSSIBILITIES CURVE: A SIMPLE, MAINSTREAM MODEL

An *economic model* is a theoretical, simplified construct designed to focus on a key set of economic relationships. Economists use models because they cannot conduct real-world experiments that isolate key factors, like scientists do, to determine how the real world functions. The best they can do is to construct a theoretical picture of how they think the economy works—a model—and then see if their model fits with what they observe happening around them. For example, as we saw in Chapter 1, economists have created a model of the demand curve which suggests that when the price of a good goes up, consumers buy less of it. This model is reasonably accurate much of the time, as we will see later.

However, models are only as good as the simplifying assumptions upon which they are based. Any failing in the underlying assumptions will render the model inaccurate. Additionally, all models are based on a major, additional *ceteris paribus assumption* that **all other relevant factors do not change.** When economists draw a demand curve showing that higher prices cause people to purchase less of a good, they have to assume, *ceteris paribus*, that consumer confidence remains unchanged (improved consumer confidence would likely mean additional consumer spending on all goods even if prices were higher) and that the product did not become a hot item (which would also increase consumer demand even if prices were higher).

To demonstrate the usefulness and limitations of economic models, we will use a *production possibilities curve (PPC)*, which is **a model that shows all combinations of 2 goods that can be produced, holding the amount of resources and the level of technology fixed.** The PPC model is designed to show the tradeoffs (opportunity costs) that occur when more of a single good is produced.

Consider the production possibilities curve in Figure 2.1, which shows all possible combinations of 2 services, Defense and Education, that the U.S. government can provide using all of its available resources and current technology. If the U.S. government decides to devote all of its available resources to defense, it would select option A, with 40 units of Defense and 0 units of Education. Or, the U.S. government could produce 100 units of Education, but this would leave no resources left to use for Defense, reducing Defense production to 0. Thus, the opportunity cost of increasing the production of Education from 0 units to 100 units, moving from point A to point D, is 40 units of Defense (what is sacrificed when the government chooses to switch all of its available resources from Defense to Education). The government can also choose to produce at any point between point

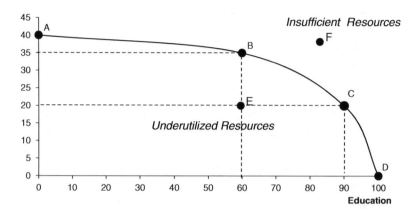

FIGURE 2.1 Production possibilities curve for U.S. government spending on Defense, Education.

Choice	Education	Defense
A	0	40
B	60	35
C	90	20
D	100	0

FIGURE 2.2 A table showing the production possibilities combinations in Figure 2.1.

A and point D on the production possibilities curve. Figure 2.2 displays the combinations of Defense and Education that the U.S. government can choose in table form, matching the options that are graphed in Figure 2.1.

Suppose that the government is currently at point B, producing 35 units of Defense and 60 units of Education. Now suppose the government decides to increase the production of Education to 90 units, moving from point B to point C. The only way they can increase the production of Education, given that they are stuck with existing resources and technology, is by reducing the production of Defense from 35 units to 20 units. The opportunity cost of moving from point B to point C would be 15 units of Defense, which is what is given up in exchange for 30 additional units of education.

The assumptions behind the PPC model include the following: (1) There are only 2 relevant goods; (2) any point on the PPC curve involves the full employment of available resources; (3) resources are fixed; (4) technology is fixed; and, (5) any other factors that might affect the production of the 2 goods in question will remain unchanged (the *ceteris paribus* assumption).

Note that any point on the PPC, including points A, B, C, and D, involves utilizing *all* of the government's available resources efficiently. If some resources were not being used, or if resources were being used inefficiently, then the U.S. government would be at a point *inside* the production possibilities curve, such as point E.

Also note that, while the U.S. government would like to be able to provide more defense and more education for its citizens, it cannot choose a point outside the PPC because it does not have sufficient resources or effective enough technology (scarcity). The only way for the U.S. government to reach point F, which is beyond the PPC, would be if it had additional resources or if there were an improvement in technology that allowed more production of both education and defense than is currently possible. Any change in the availability of resources or technology, however, would be a change in the assumptions behind the model, and we would have to draw a new PPC reflecting the new assumptions.

2.3 THE SPECIALIZATION OF RESOURCES

The shape of the production possibilities curve is also important. The PPC above has a downward (negative) slope that becomes steeper and steeper (it is concave to the origin). This occurs whenever a PPC reflects the *specialization of resources*: **When some resources cannot be easily adapted from one use to another.** For example, some resources that are used to produce Defense, such as tanks and bombers, are not well-suited for producing Education. Similarly, some resources that are used to produce Education, such as schools and school buses, are poorly suited for producing Defense.

We can see the specialization of resources in the PPC in Figure 2.1 and in the table in Figure 2.2 when the amounts of Education exchanged for Defense vary. If we begin at point A, the government is producing all Defense and no Education. Even schools, buses and teachers are being used for national defense! Now suppose that the government decides to shift some resources out of Defense and into Education, moving from point A to point B. They will, of course, shift the resources most specialized for education first. By shifting the schools, buses and teachers from producing Defense to producing Education, the result is very little loss in Defense (5 units) for a very large gain in Education (60 units). Between point A and point B, 5 units of Defense (*D*) use the same resources that could produce 60 units of Education (*E*). To put this in mathematical terms:

From A – B, $5D = 60E$

Dividing both sides by 5 to find the opportunity cost of 1 unit of defense, we get:

From A – B, $(5 / 5)D = (60 / 5)E$; and $1D = 12E$

From A to B, each unit of Defense sacrificed results in 12 units of Education being produced.

Now suppose that the government wants to devote even more resources to Education. Moving from B to C involves producing 30 additional units of Education while giving up 15 units of Defense. The resources that were best suited for Education were already shifted into Education when the government moved from A to B. Now the government is shifting resources that are well-suited for either Defense or for Education. This would include soldiers who could also be teachers, computers, and equipment that could be used for education or for defense, and so on. Now the opportunity cost of each unit is different. From point B to point C, 15 units of Defense (D) are given up for 30 units of Education (E). In mathematical terms,

From $B - C, 15D = 30E$; and if we divide both sides by $15, 1D = 2E$.

Similarly, if the government moves from point C to point D, 20 units of Defense are given up in exchange for only 10 units of Education. Now the government is shifting all of their resources into Education, even those that are well suited for Defense but very poorly suited for Education, such as bombs, bombers, tanks, and guns.

From $C - D, 10E = 20D$; and $1D = \frac{1}{2}E.$

From C to D, each unit of Defense that is given up only results in half of a unit of Education ($\frac{1}{2}$ E) being produced.

The last column in Figure 2.3 shows how the opportunity cost of 1 unit of Defense changes as the government moves from point A to point D.

Similarly, we can compute the opportunity cost of one unit of Education in each region of the PPC, which you can see in the fifth column of the table in Figure 2.3.

The change in the opportunity cost of one unit of each good on a curved production possibilities curve displays something mainstream

Choice	Education	Defense	Opportunity Cost	Opportunity Cost of 1 unit of Education	Opportunity Cost of 1 Unit of Defense
A	0	40			
A-B			60E = 5D	1E = (1/12)D	1D = 12E
B	60	35			
B-C			30E = 15D	1E = (1/2)D	1D = 2E
C	90	20			
C-D			10E = 20D	1E = 2D	1D = (1/2)E
D	100	0			

FIGURE 2.3 Changes in opportunity cost due to the specialization of resources.

economists refer to as the *law of increasing opportunity cost*: **If resources are specialized and if all resources are being used efficiently, then, as more and more of a particular good is produced, the opportunity cost of producing each additional unit of that good will increase.** In other words, as we produce more and more units of Education, moving from point A to point D on the PPC in Figure 2.1, each unit of Education will have a higher opportunity cost. This occurs because we have to give up more and more units of Defense to get one unit of Education as we shift resources that are better suited to Defense into the production of Education. This situation also works in reverse: As we produce more and more units of Defense, moving from point D to point A on the PPC in Figure 2.1, each unit of Defense has a higher opportunity cost because we are shifting resources into Defense that are better suited to Education as we get closer to point A.

There are some important real-world examples of the law of increasing opportunity cost at work. For instance, in the 1980s, the Soviet Union devoted about 17 percent of its economy to national defense. The Soviet Union collapsed in 1990, ending the Cold War in which the U.S. and the Soviet Union built up huge military arsenals. The Soviet Union became Russia and a group of independent countries. Russian officials decided to reduce the size of their military to 3 percent of the economy and shift from the production of defense into the production of consumer goods, energy, health care, and other non-defense items that Russia needed. They hoped to see a huge boom in other sectors as they shifted resources out of defense. But the boom was much smaller than they anticipated. Why? One of the biggest reasons was the specialization of resources: All of the huge defense factories and specialized defense workers who built tanks and served as soldiers were not very productive when it came to producing non-defense goods. After 1990, Russia sacrificed a vast amount of defense in exchange for a much smaller increase in the production of non-defense goods.

Recently, T. Boone Pickens has proposed that the U.S. stop using so much imported oil by converting automobiles to use U.S.-produced compressed natural gas. It is an interesting proposal, but due to the specialization of resources, we must consider carefully the opportunity cost of doing so. The transportation infrastructure in the U.S. is built around using gasoline made from oil; converting all of the cars, gas stations, and refineries to produce compressed natural gas would be difficult and expensive—and would come with a significant opportunity cost.

The above examples all refer to cases in which resources are specialized. However, if resources are not specialized, then opportunity costs would be constant along a PPC rather than increasing, and the PPC would be a straight line. For example, Figure 2.4 shows a production possibilities curve for a company producing black shoes and brown shoes. Since the

Brown Shoes

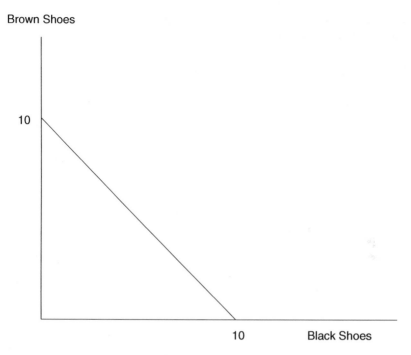

FIGURE 2.4 A PPC without specialized resources.

only difference between the shoes is the color of the dye used, resources (labor, machinery, etc.) can be shifted easily from the production of black shoes to the production of brown shoes.

2.4 SHIFTS IN THE PRODUCTION POSSIBILITIES CURVE

A production possibilities curve is drawn based on the assumption that resources and technology are fixed. But what would happen if more resources or better technology were made available? We would need to draw a new PPC that is shifted outward. The type of shift would depend on whether or not the resources or technology were better suited for the production of one good or both goods.

For example, consider an economy producing Cars and Food. If better robots were invented that can produce either item, then the PPC would shift out, showing that society can now have more of both goods. This is shown in example (a) in Figure 2.5. What if the newly invented robots can only be used to produce Cars? Then the PPC shifts out on the "Cars" axis, but not on the "Food" axis, as shown in Figure 2.5, example (b).

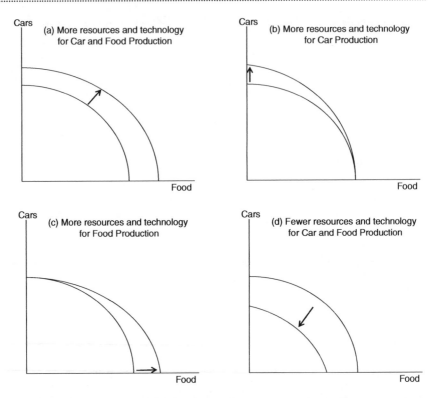

FIGURE 2.5 Shifts in the PPC from changes in resources or technology.

If the robots could only be used for producing Food, the PPC would shift out only on the "Food" axis, as shown in Figure 2.5, example (c). Finally, suppose that a natural disaster reduced the resources available for Food and Car production. The result would be a PPC that has shifted in on both axes, as shown in Figure 2.5, example (d).

2.5 CAPITAL GOODS, CONSUMER GOODS, AND ECONOMIC GROWTH

One of the key issues in determining whether or not an economy (and its PPC) grows is the priority that the people in an economy give to generating productive resources. *Capital goods* are **the machinery, equipment, buildings, and productive resources (other than labor) used to produce goods and services.** When an economy produces capital goods, it becomes more productive, shifting out its PPC. A PPC could also shift out from an improvement in **technology**, which would make capital goods more productive. **Labor** is another productive resource. When an economy has more laborers, it can produce more goods and services, shifting out its PPC. Economists also consider **human capital** to be a capital good: Education and training make our labor force more productive, which also shifts out the PPC. *Consumer goods*, on the other hand, are **goods that are purchased and used by consumers, but that do not contribute to future productivity.** Consumer goods include such items as beer, clothing, and food. The addition of labor, human capital, or capital goods increases an economy's productivity and shifts out its PPC, but producing additional consumer goods does not shift the PPC.

Mainstream economic theory suggests that, in general, economic growth (growth in the PPC) is a result of increases in labor, increases in capital goods, and increases in productivity (from better technology or greater human capital):

Economic Growth $= \Delta L + \Delta K + \Delta$Productivity

where $\Delta=$ change, L=Labor, and K=Capital.

An economy that draws more of its population into the labor force, devotes more of its resources to capital goods than to consumer goods, and improves its education and technology will experience more rapid economic growth.

Much of China's recent growth can be explained by these factors: For the last 35 years, China drew millions of relatively unproductive rural workers into its highly productive urban factories, and it invested heavily in capital goods, technology development, education, and infrastructure (roads, bridges, ports, and airports, also considered capital goods), which in turn increased productivity. The result was an astounding economic boom and economic growth averaging 9.8 percent a year from 1979–2013. For comparison, the average annual U.S. economic growth rate during the same period was 2.7 percent.

Defense spending and growth

Interestingly, government spending on national defense is considered to be a consumer good. Defense spending protects people within a country, but it does not increase the economy's productive capacity. Thus, we "consume" defense much like we do other services that we value but that do not contribute to economic growth.

Consider Figure 2.6, which shows a PPC for capital goods and consumer goods. If the society depicted in Figure 2.6 chooses point A, with more capital goods and fewer consumer goods like national defense, it will experience greater economic growth, its PPC will shift out further, and it will have a higher standard of living in the future (a larger PPC which

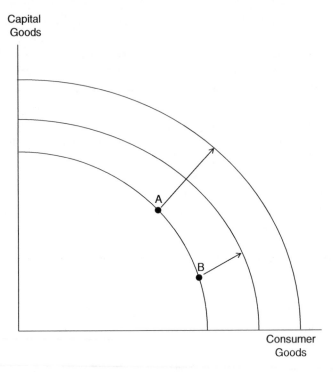

FIGURE 2.6 Growth in the PPC from more capital goods.

allows it to consume more of both goods). If the society chooses point B, with fewer capital goods and more consumer goods, the PPC will shift out less in the future.

The facts that economic growth is generated in part by capital goods and that defense spending is a consumer good make the choice of whether or not to devote significant resources to national defense a very important one for a society. As you can see in Figure 2.7, the United States devotes more of its resources to military spending than any other country in the world. In fact, the U.S. devotes more money to defense than the next 7 countries combined! The U.S. spends twice as much on defense as the countries the U.S. sees as major security risks: China, Russia, Iran, and North Korea. The opportunity cost of spending so much on defense is both the current goods that are given up *and* the future goods that are sacrificed due to lower economic growth.

Thus, the mainstream PPC model focuses on how society chooses to allocate its scarce resources. In doing so, the model encourages society to consider carefully the opportunity costs of making choices. However, as we will see in the next section, political economists extend their analysis of scarcity and choice into additional areas.

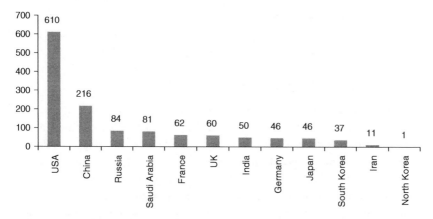

FIGURE 2.7 10 largest military spenders in 2014, plus Iran, and North Korea, in billions of $.

2.6 A POLITICAL ECONOMY CRITIQUE OF SCARCITY AND CHOICE IN MAINSTREAM ECONOMICS

The economies of the modern developed world produce enough goods and services for everyone to have a standard of living that would have been unthinkable a century ago. Thus, to characterize economics as the study of scarcity rather than abundance is a reflection of a particular set of assumptions and value choices. To mainstream economists, an efficient allocation of resources occurs when no one can be made better off without making someone else worse off. The idea of redistributing goods and services from one person to another is considered outside of the realm of analysis. This is a reflection of the mainstream's attempt to practice value-free, "positive" analysis rather than taking into consideration values and other normative elements of economic issues. Political economists of various types find the mainstream analysis of scarcity and choice overly limiting, and they extend their analysis into a number of areas, including ethics, culture, underemployment of resources, inequality, and gender empowerment. A brief analysis of each of these areas will provide an excellent introduction to the crucial differences between mainstream analysis and that of different schools of political economy.

Ethical considerations

Social economists urge us to consider the ethical considerations of our decisions regarding resource allocation. Is it ethical to devote additional resources to B-2 bombers and other defense goods when many children do not have enough food to eat? One of the most important economic decisions a society can make is how it chooses to allocate its resources, and such ethical considerations play a crucial part in that choice.

Culture and conspicuous consumption

The fact that rich consumers in wealthy countries want to buy more and more lavish goods can be seen as an indication not of scarcity but of what the **institutionalist** economist Thorstein Veblen called *conspicuous consumption*: **Purchasing goods in order to display social status.** To Veblen and other institutionalists, a crucial aspect of an economic system is the cultural forces that encourage conspicuous consumption at the expense of other worthwhile societal goals. Why do human beings seem bent on showing off their wealth to achieve social status? From this perspective, understanding consumer choices is less about scarcity than the fact that consumers with an unprecedented level of material well-being, drowning in high tech gadgets and luxury goods, think that they need to buy even more goods than they already have. Determining the cultural processes that drive consumerist attitudes is therefore important to our understanding of resource allocation in the economy.

Underemployed resources

Another issue concerns whether or not resources are ever fully employed, and how easily they can be switched to new uses. The production possibilities curve model implies that resources are usually fully employed and that resources can always be shifted to another use; although, there may be increasing opportunity costs when that is done. Does this match the real world experiences we see around us? As U.S. manufacturers have increasingly moved their factories to foreign sites in China, Mexico, and elsewhere, there has been a significant increase in availability of resources. Buildings, factories, machines, and manufacturing workers in the U.S. are now available to produce different goods instead of the steel, cars, and other manufactured goods that they used to produce. However, instead of shifting easily and quickly into other productive activities, most of the old factories sit unused, and many manufacturing workers remain unemployed. The "rust belt" of the U.S., with depressed cities like Detroit, Youngstown, and Allentown, shows us that the shift of resources to new uses has not happened effectively. In reality, given chronic unemployment and underutilized resources, the U.S. may never have been on its PPC. From a **post-Keynesian** perspective, the key economic problem is not scarcity but how society can put all of its productive resources to their best possible use. In every society, there are people who need work and work that needs to be done. The key economic issue is not so much scarcity as the underemployment of resources, something that can be addressed by good government policies.

Inequality

It is also worth pointing out that abundance for the few is accompanied in wealthy countries by vast poverty. At the same time that the rich are consuming ever more luxury goods, more than 1.5 million people experience homelessness in a single year in the U.S. To a **Marxist** economist, the key issue is not scarcity but the structure of the class system and power structures of society that result in abundance for a few and poverty and homelessness for millions. Why are the lower classes in the U.S., and especially citizens from Black and Latino backgrounds, so poor while others are so rich? Scarcity, from a Marxist perspective, is a condition imposed on the working class by greedy capitalists who want more for themselves while denying workers a decent standard of living. Only in countries where strong labor movements have reduced the power of corporate interests do we see workers earning a decent share of what is produced. Marxists focus on the analysis of social classes to understand resource allocation in societies, a topic that is omitted from mainstream analysis.

Gender empowerment

Another key issue, from the perspective of **feminist** economists, involves who is making the decisions and what priorities their decisions reflect. If women had greater political and economic power, would the decisions of society reflect different priorities? The northern European countries that lead the world in gender empowerment tend to have much more generous family leave policies and welfare states. They provide new parents with up to a year of paid leave to care for a child (compared with 6 weeks of unpaid leave in the U.S.), and they provide all citizens with high quality health care and education (including college), paid for by taxes on income and consumption. These countries have decided to devote more resources to family time, health, and education, while devoting fewer resources to consumer goods. There is a gendered component to decision-making that reflects crucial aspects of an economic system, so any analysis of resource allocation must include an analysis of gender.

The above examples of how various groups of political economists view scarcity and choice illustrate the fundamental difference between mainstream economics and political economy: Mainstream economists prefer focusing on specific decisions using the concepts of scarcity and opportunity cost, while political economists prefer a **much broader approach** that emphasizes various crucial **institutions** in the economy. That approach is described in more detail in the next section.

2.7 INSTITUTIONAL ANALYSIS: A POLITICAL ECONOMY APPROACH TO THE STUDY OF RESOURCE ALLOCATION

When political economists study resource allocation they focus on institutions. *Institutions* are **the organizations, social structures, rules, and habits that structure human interactions and the economy.** Formal institutions include the laws, regulations, firms, government bodies, and the political system. Informal institutions include culture, social classes, habits, and other patterns of behavior that shape how people act and interact. Institutions are specific to a particular time and place. From this perspective, the opportunity cost of producing bombers is less informative than the factors that shape the actual choice of bombers and national defense over education in the modern U.S.

In analyzing why the U.S. has chosen to devote vast resources to B-2 Bombers and other defense goods over education, political economists focus on power structures, class, politics, culture, and other key institutions. The economic system in the modern U.S. is dominated by huge corporations. Similarly, the political system is dominated to a large degree by those corporations and the wealthy individuals who own them, and who give vast sums of money to politicians. Some of the most powerful corporations and wealthy individuals have financial interests in the defense industry, and via political donations they encourage politicians to keep building B-2 bombers. U.S. corporate interests in foreign countries sometimes need the U.S. military to intervene on their behalf, which requires a U.S. military presence around the globe. In general, political economists see the U.S. military as supporting the dominant class of corporate leaders, wealthy owners, and politicians.

The U.S. military is itself a powerful institution which has been very successful in persuading Congress to continue funding defense expenditures at an extremely high level, even in times of peace. Furthermore, Congress can safely spend huge sums of money on defense due in part to U.S. cultural attitudes. The U.S. is known to be much more patriotic than other countries, as measured in the World Values Surveys. This contributes to a willingness of citizens to devote more resources to the military than other countries do, and the ability of politicians to appeal to patriotism when they increase funding for national defense.

These factors led President Dwight D. Eisenhower, a 5-star general during World War II, to warn against the powerful alliance of the corporate defense industry and the military. In a famous speech in 1961, he warned, "In the councils of government, we must guard against the acquisition of unwarranted influence, whether sought or unsought, by the military-industrial complex. The potential for the disastrous rise of misplaced power exists, and will persist." The fact that defense spending in the U.S. continues to be at a level much higher than other countries indicates the ongoing vitality of the military-industrial complex.

From a political economy perspective, the decision of the U.S. to place a very high priority on national defense and a lower priority on education in comparison to most developed countries is a product of a variety of institutional factors. Scarcity is one of the important issues that affects how many resources can be devoted to defense and education. Nonetheless, political economists prefer a much broader focus for economics than scarcity. Economic models can be useful in helping us to focus on a few key economic relationships, but they can ignore many other important factors that come into play. The question of which relationships to focus on deeply divides mainstream and political economists.

2.8 CONCLUSION

To mainstream economists, economics is about the difficult choices an individual, firm, or society must make when resources are scarce. By carefully considering the opportunity cost as well as the benefits of choosing to devote resources in a particular way, decision-making can be improved. A simple mainstream model, the production possibilities curve, can be used to analyze the opportunity cost of a particular allocation of resources, including the relationship between capital goods, consumer goods, and economic growth. This is a flexible approach that can be applied to numerous situations.

Political economists acknowledge the usefulness of cost-benefit analysis, while also stressing the need to broaden this approach. From a political economy perspective, economists must go beyond scarcity to study the institutions that shape choices in a society. By combining the focused cost-benefit analysis of mainstream economics with the breadth of political economy, you are likely to get a very clear picture of the tradeoffs facing society and how those tradeoffs are shaped by key institutional factors.

To be sure, the analysis above is but a quick glance at a set of different approaches taken by mainstream and political economists. As we continue, these differences will become more apparent. Also, it is important to recognize that the example of the mainstream PPC model suggests a fundamental focus by the mainstream on mathematical approaches and an attempt to make their analysis as scientific as possible. Political economists, on the other hand, prefer to bring in additional factors that cannot always be measured precisely but which, nevertheless, can have an important influence on the economy.

Now that you are familiar with some of the fundamental premises and applications of mainstream economics and political economy, the next crucial topic to explore is the evolution of the global economy over time. The institutions of society were developed in the past and shape the future in key ways. The best way to understand where the economic system is going is to understand where it has been. Analyzing economic history can help you anticipate the likely trends in the future, and such economic forecasting is an invaluable economic skill.

QUESTIONS FOR REVIEW

1. Explain how each of the following events would affect scarcity.
    a. Consumers' desire for goods and services decreases.
    b. Resources become less plentiful.
    c. The government discovers a large amount of unused resources.
2. Use the concept of opportunity cost to analyze the decision of whether or not you should study economics tonight.
3. The graph below in Figure 2.8 displays a production possibilities curve for the World in choosing between allocating resources to Food or Machinery.
    a. What is the opportunity cost of moving from point B to point D?

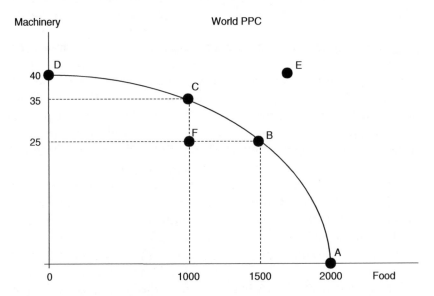

FIGURE 2.8 PPC for Problem 3.

  b. What is the opportunity cost of 1 unit of Machinery between point D and point C?

  c. Which points on the graph are considered to be efficient and feasible? Explain briefly.

  d. The reason for the curved shape of the PPC above is that (choose the best answer):

   (a) Resources are scarce.

   (b) Increasing food production causes a decrease in machinery production.

   (c) There are opportunity costs for producing more of either good.

   (d) Some inputs are better at producing food than machinery.

   (e) None of the above.

  e. Scientists estimate that global climate change will destroy 10% of land that is current used to produce Food. Show on a graph how this will affect the PPC.

  f. Assuming that the World is at point B on the PPC, producing and consuming 1500 units of Food, and that the World will need to continue consuming the same amount after global climate change destroys 10% of land, how will the destruction of land affect the production of Machinery? Will economic growth in the future be affected by these changes? Why or why not?

  g. How would political economists broaden the analysis in parts e and f of this question? What institutions would they think are most relevant to the issues being raised?

4. The graph in Figure 2.9 displays a production possibilities curve for the U.S. in choosing between allocating resources to Transportation or Beer.

  a. What is the opportunity cost of 1 unit of Beer between point A and point B?

  b. What is the opportunity cost of moving from point A to point C?

  c. Show what would happen to the graph if the government fails to maintain their transportation infrastructure.

  d. The President of the U.S. recently proposed that the U.S. should dramatically increase its transportation spending. Assume that the economy is currently at point B in Figure 2.9. If we follow the President's plan and increase transportation spending dramatically, what would be the immediate, short-term effect?

  e. Economic data indicate that transportation spending by the government improves businesses' productivity. Using the PPC model, analyze what the President's proposal to increase transportation spending will do in the long run to the U.S. economy.

  f. How would political economists respond to the analysis in parts d and e?

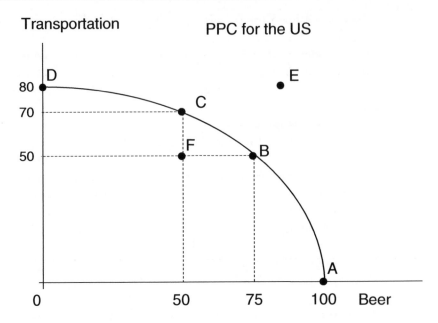

FIGURE 2.9 PPC for Problem 4.

5. Given the factors that mainstream economists believe contribute to economic growth, what would happen to economic growth and to the production possibilities curve for the U.S. if it halts all immigration into the country and the U.S. population actually declines?

6. Scientists are convinced that the burning of fossil fuels is contributing to global climate change, which will harm future economic growth.

   a. Construct a PPC showing the tradeoff between fossil fuels and renewable energy. Explain how different points on the PPC will affect future growth in the PPC.

   b. Undertake an analysis from a political economy perspective about the choice of whether or not to devote resources to renewable energy. Why do you think the U.S. devotes fewer resources to renewable energy than many other developed countries?

PART II

The evolution of economic ideas and systems

The economic systems of the world have changed dramatically over the course of human history. The only certainty about economic systems appears to be that they will continue to change as they are forced to confront inherent contradictions and new problems. Human economic systems evolved from cooperative hunting and gathering communities to kingdoms that exploited slaves to variations of market capitalism in which privately owned firms controlled the bulk of society's resources. The fact that no economic system has lasted forever leads to an interesting question: *What type of economic system might replace contemporary market capitalism?*

As economic systems evolved, so did economic thought. All economic thinkers reflect the society and the economic problems of their era. Some of the earliest authors who took up economic topics, including Plato and Aristotle, justified slavery on the grounds that some people were naturally inferior. Adam Smith lived towards the end of the mercantilist era, when giant monopolies working with autocratic governments dominated global trade and extracted resources from the rest of society. He believed that unregulated market capitalism would be preferable to mercantilism because competition would limit the power of monopolistic firms and enhance the wellbeing of workers. Karl Marx wrote during the dark ages of capitalism, when it was not uncommon for children to be shackled to machines for up to 78 hours a week. Marx hoped that a socialist or communist system would solve the worst excesses of capitalism. In the early 1900s, Thorstein Veblen saw small U.S. firms were being displaced by vast corporations run by the robber barons, who ruthlessly extracted profits from their workers and from society. Like Smith, Veblen believed that only by reining in large corporations would market capitalism be able to function for the wellbeing of all people. John Maynard Keynes wrote his masterwork, *The General Theory of Employment, Interest and Money*, during the Great Depression, a crisis which convinced him and many others that unregulated market capitalism could not work. Keynes advocated a regulated form of capitalism, which is the economic system that came to dominate the modern world. But, as Keynes was advocating the development of a government-regulated market capitalist economy, the rise of Hitler in Germany and Stalin in the Soviet Union caused Friedrich Hayek to question whether or not we should put our trust in government.

Part II describes the evolution of economic systems from ancient times to the present. In the process, we will take up the best ideas of the most influential economists in the context in which they wrote their ideas. As we study the different forms that economic systems have taken, think carefully about what lessons emerge regarding human nature from the many ways in which human beings have organized themselves to produce the goods and services necessary for survival. And, as we study the theories of the great economists, critically evaluate their ideas against the economy you see around you to decide for yourself which theories are still relevant to the modern world.

Chapter 3 investigates the evolution of economic systems from communal, tribal societies to slave-based empires, followed by feudalism and mercantilism. Chapter 4 describes the establishment of capitalism and the ideas of Adam Smith. Chapter 5 goes through the labor unrest and economic crises that were a product of the dark ages of capitalism in the mid-1800s, and the ideas that Karl Marx developed during this period. Chapter 6 describes the ideas of Thorstein Veblen, and the rise of monopoly capitalism which culminated in the Great Depression and the fall of laissez-faire. Chapter 7 describes the rise of mixed market capitalism based on the ideas of John Maynard Keynes. Part II concludes with Chapter 8, which examines the market dominated, social market and state dominated economies we see in the modern world.

The evolution of pre-capitalist economic systems

From communal societies to empires, feudalism, and mercantilism

Every society needs an economic system of some sort to provide the goods and services its people need to survive and thrive. But only in modern times, under capitalism, has that economy been controlled by markets and the pursuit of private profit. Early human societies did make use of markets, but their use was extremely limited and markets were almost never entrusted with the provision of the main goods that a society needed for its survival.

The harsh conditions of the ancient world required people to band together for survival. The survival of individuals required doing everything necessary for the group to insure its survival. The largest, most closely knit groups were the ones that triumphed over smaller, less cohesive ones. Thus, due to our evolutionary history, individual motivations seem to be group-oriented rather than completely self-interested. This is one of the biggest reasons why political economists dispute the mainstream economics portrayal of economic man as primarily individualistic and self-interested: Throughout human history people have cared deeply about their place in their social group. In fact, their survival depended on it.

Human beings have lived and worked in a wide variety of economic systems, which they have designed over the centuries. As we will see below, early human societies were usually characterized by reciprocity, redistribution, sharing, and trust. They also engaged in some specialization of tasks and a simple division of labor to facilitate their survival.

Once societies began to produce enough surplus food that everyone did not have to work, hierarchical class systems began to develop. These grew in size and complexity as the surplus expanded, accompanied by a gradual increase in the use of trade and markets to provide goods for the elites. In slave societies, a small minority controlled the resources, and most of the population barely earned enough to survive. However, slave societies proved to be unstable, and they were followed by the static, hierarchical system of feudalism, where lords controlled the labor of serfs. Feudalism lasted for 1000 years, but it too eventually became untenable, and it was replaced by mercantilism in the 1500s. Markets began to take on an important role when kings and merchants constructed and expanded markets for their own benefit. But even under mercantilism, markets did not control the allocation of a majority of society's resources. It was only with the advent of full-fledged capitalism in the 1800s that market capitalism became the dominant economic system and society's productive resources, land, labor, and capital came to be allocated by markets.

This chapter will describe the evolution of human economic systems from communal, tribal societies to the more hierarchical systems of slave-based empires, feudalism and mercantilism. It draws on the classic work by Karl Polanyi, *The Great Transformation*, along with recent discoveries in economic anthropology, psychology, and evolutionary biology that address the evolution of human societies over time.

3.0 CHAPTER 3 LEARNING GOALS

After reading this chapter you should be able to:

- Outline the main characteristics of (1) traditional, hunter-gatherer societies; (2) slave-based empires (Rome); (3) feudalism and (4) mercantilism; and describe the common threads and major differences of these human societies;
- Analyze the role of tradition, authority, and markets, along with the specialization of labor and the use of the surplus product, in each of these four economic systems;
- Explain how cooperation, specialization, redistribution, and reciprocity were important to the survival of people living in hunter-gatherer societies and in other economic systems;
- Describe the types of social classes and role of private property in the different economic systems; and,

- List and analyze the major forces that eroded each economic system and paved the way for the next economic system.

We begin by considering what we know about the earliest human societies that existed.

3.1 TRADITIONAL ECONOMIES: ANCIENT HUNTER-GATHERER SOCIETIES

So, what were the earliest economic systems like?

Human beings are inherently group-oriented, social creatures. Archaeological evidence indicates that the earliest tool-using human ancestors of 2 million years ago were nomadic hunter-gatherers living in groups of around 70 members, usually formed by large kinship groups (extended families). It is worth analyzing why working in groups was essential to survival because this helps us to understand how we evolved as a group-oriented species.

The earliest human societies lived on the edge of survival. They did not have the ability to store food for long periods, so obtaining a steady supply of food every day was the primary human activity. Any shortfall for a sustained period of time meant starvation. In this environment, cooperative communities had an advantage while individuals or very small groups usually did not last long.

Cooperation was useful in protecting the community from predators, including animals as well as other human groups. A larger community could also engage in larger scale, risky activities. While some community members were devoted to the regular hunting and gathering activities, some high-risk endeavors with potentially large payoffs, such as hunting large game, would be undertaken by a small portion of the community. This allowed for a degree of **specialization** and innovation in performing tasks and resulted in a more secure food supply.

Redistribution (sharing) and **reciprocity** within the group were defining characteristics of these early societies. As Karl Polanyi observes in *The Great Transformation*, "The Bergdama returning from his hunting excursion, the woman coming back from her search for roots, fruit, or leaves are expected to offer the greater part of their spoil for the benefit of the community." Producers share with their community because they can expect reciprocity: When another member of the community finds food, they too will share it.

Redistribution was crucial to survival in that a family without the support of a larger group was at high risk of starvation. One bout of serious illness or a run of bad luck in hunting and gathering and the family could starve. However, with the support of the community, they could survive the lean times. Thus, while independent families did sometimes live on their own (householding), it was the larger groups that were more successful.

Sometimes chiefs controlled the method of redistribution in larger groups, and sometimes redistribution was done based on traditional social roles. This type of system has sometimes been labeled **primitive communism** because of the emphasis on common production and the relatively egalitarian sharing of the collectively produced goods.

To effectively allocate tasks and goods, our human ancestors developed customs or traditions. A *traditional economy* is one in which **resources are allocated based on communal patterns of reciprocity and redistribution, and in which tasks are allocated and knowledge and skills preserved through established social relationships.** In this sense, a traditional economy is dominated by the cultural forces that shape the allocation of resources, goods, and tasks. In such societies, culture and tradition were crucial in making sure society's knowledge was passed down to the next generation, guaranteeing that a community had enough people with the appropriate skill set allocated to each task (hunting, tracking, gathering, tool making, etc.), and in uniting society in the face of external threats.

Anthropologists have been able to observe hunter-gatherer societies that have survived until the modern era, and they have seen redistributive and reciprocal behaviors firsthand. For example, Pierre Robbe describes the Inuit dividing up the meat from a bear that had been killed:

> Virtually all the inhabitants of the village were there, standing around the animal in three roughly concentric circles: Harald [the first person to see the bear] and the five participants (those who had been members of the hunt), then the other men of the village who were going to take part in the cutting up of the bear... and finally the women and the children.

Although more of the bear meat goes to the person who spotted the bear and to those who killed the bear, some must be shared with the entire community. We see similar methods of redistribution in other societies, with all hunters and gatherers sharing what they find or kill with the community according to established social rules.

In the harsh hunter-gatherer environment, the highest social status was given to those who were the most productive members of society. One of the characteristics of people in all human societies seems to be the desire to achieve social status. The desire for status is probably hard-wired into us by the evolutionary process: Those who achieved a higher social status were more likely to survive and procreate. Historical evidence indicates that human beings are inherently *status-seeking*, which is **the human propensity to strive to achieve the highest social status possible, given the values of the community in which they live.**

The criteria for achieving a high social status varies substantially based on the society and its priorities. Traditional economies valued the production of food and held the most productive hunters and gatherers in high esteem. Some traditional societies also developed elaborate systems of gift-giving as displays of status. As ethnologist Marcel Mauss observed in his classic work, *The Gift*, these communities engaged in a competitive exchanging of gifts in which gift-givers tried to outdo others in order to achieve social status. A modern parallel would be some countries in Europe, Asia, and the Middle East in which generous gestures to others, such as paying for the entire group's dinner and drinks when dining out, is considered an act worthy of esteem and praise. In contrast, capitalist economies tend to celebrate the accumulation of personal wealth. To political economists, one of the keys to analyzing the economy of a particular place is understanding how its culture shapes the status-seeking of its members. Human beings work to succeed in their particular community, which means they try to **act rationally within a cultural context** to achieve social status.

In addition to valuing productivity above other activities, most traditional communities tended to practice a form of direct democracy. Each adult had a say in major decisions, so the power of the chief was quite limited.

In such communities, there was limited specialization of tasks. Everyone needed to perform a large number of tasks every day just to stay alive. The most significant division of tasks was along gender lines, with men performing the hunting and women focused on gathering, child-rearing, and cooking. Mothers would teach their daughters the knowledge and skills associated with their specialized tasks, and their daughters would follow in their footsteps. Fathers and sons followed the same pattern.

The development of technology was severely limited because traditional economies produced barely enough food to survive and because of the limited amount of specialization. *Technology* refers to **the tools, skills, and scientific knowledge that society develops in the use of resources to produce goods and services.** Technology, along with cultural factors, plays a crucial role in structuring what an economic system is like. Societies that face a constant threat of starvation tend to be deeply risk averse, and they are rarely willing to expend the labor and resources necessary to develop new technologies. Nor do they have enough surplus labor or resources to undertake substantial investments in new technologies due to their low level of productivity.

Despite these limitations, archaeological evidence has proven that human groups steadily increased in size over time, indicating that larger groups had an evolutionary advantage over smaller groups. As noted above, larger groups can have a greater degree of specialization of labor. *Specialization of labor* is a fundamental characteristic of all human societies in which **particular tasks are performed by specific individuals, rather than everyone performing all tasks.** Specialization tends to improve productivity because people develop **skills,** becoming very good at the tasks they specialize in (tracking game, finding roots and berries, etc.). Via their expertise, they can develop simple **tools** (technology) for their work. The larger the group, the more specialized the tasks that can exist, and the more productive that society is likely to be. Furthermore, larger groups have greater **military power** and are better able to dominate smaller groups. Correspondingly, those humans who could successfully function in large groups were more likely to survive. Our evolutionary past indicates that we evolved to function effectively in a large group setting.

For many thousands of years, human economies continued to be dominated by traditions that specified who would undertake which tasks; how food, tools, and other resources would be used and shared; and who would achieve the highest status in the community based on his or her productivity. Human groups faced increasing pressures to grow larger in size in order to increase their military power, which necessitated improvements in productivity (via specialization and risk-taking) to produce more food to support a larger population.

The invention of agriculture and food storage ushered in a new era of human development, involving settled life and the establishment of villages, towns, and even cities. The importance of being successful in a large group became even more crucial as societies grew larger and more complex.

3.2 AGRICULTURE AND THE ESTABLISHMENT OF CITIES, SOCIAL CLASSES, AND SLAVE-BASED EMPIRES

About 12,000 years ago, the invention of agriculture (farming and herding), sharper tools, and new materials—especially pottery for food storage—caused a dramatic increase in the ability of communities to support a larger population due to the larger supply of food.

Instead of providing subsistence just for themselves and their family, farmers were now able to produce enough food to provide for more people. In the harsh climates of sub-Saharan Africa, it took about 6 farmers to produce enough food to provide for themselves and 1 additional adult, who no longer needed to grow food and could concentrate on other things. In the more fertile regions of the Middle East, 2 farm families could support 1 non-farm family. In all agricultural regions, farming could support a larger population than had been previously possible due to the increase in productivity.

As groups grew larger, it became important to develop institutions, including codes of behavior and other rules, to develop the high degree of trust that is crucial to the functioning of a larger society. The development of a strong group identity, with cultural or religious bonds and a prevailing ideology, took on increased significance.

The importance of group identification was now even more crucial because the production and storage of surplus food made warfare increasingly important. In earlier hunter-gatherer societies, taking over another group had little benefit since they possessed little of value. In agricultural societies, however, the rewards of military aggression were substantial. A powerful army could seize the stored food and the most productive land of other groups. Then the army could force the conquered people to work as slaves and seize any surplus that was produced. This highlights a key aspect of all economic systems, the production and allocation of **surplus product**.

The *surplus product* is the amount that is produced over and above what is needed for the community's survival. The *necessary product*, what is necessary for a community's survival, includes food and shelter for everyone, plus the replacement of tools and materials used up in production.

The generation of surplus product caused dramatic changes in society. In addition to causing warfare, surpluses were as a source economic growth when they were used to augment the productive resources of society (investment). For example, excess grain that was used to feed horses or oxen, which could be used as draft animals, made farms more productive. Labor could be used to build irrigation canals and aqueducts to increase crop yields. In these cases, sacrificing current resources (grain and labor) in the short term to invest in the development of capital goods caused increased output in the future.

Surplus product was also necessary for cities to develop, since larger population centers relied on the surplus food produced by the agricultural areas for their sustenance. In those cities, artisans specialized in the development of more sophisticated tools, which increased productivity further. Human civilization as we know it grew out of the production of surplus food.

In all economic systems, **how much surplus product is generated and how it is allocated has a large impact on economic growth.** Hunter-gatherer societies had little or no surplus, so they could not invest time and resources into more elaborate endeavors; they had to concentrate on finding food. Agricultural societies could devote their surplus to raising draft animals, building irrigation systems, or developing tools (capital goods), which would increase their productivity and economic growth. Or, they could devote their surplus to amassing vast conquering armies, building temples and monuments like the pyramids of ancient Egypt or the Coliseum in Rome, and supporting an idle religious or noble class.

Control of surpluses proved to be a major source of power. The surplus of food allowed a more elaborate social hierarchy to develop in which some members of society no longer had to work to produce food. Kings, emperors, chiefs, and priests seized and controlled the land and resources, sitting atop the hierarchy and avoiding manual labor while slaves or peasants did the most productive tasks of society. With the advent of agriculture in 10,000 BCE, property rights came into existence for the first time in human history. *Property rights* exist when **a productive resource such as land or slave labor belongs to a particular person or group instead of to society as a whole**. The production of surplus is therefore also associated with the rise of private property and the establishment of social classes in human society. In economics, *class* refers to **a group of people that has a specific relationship with the production process**.

In order to protect property rights, stave off slave revolts, fend off invaders, provide public goods (irrigation, flood control, roads, etc.), and organize larger and more complex societies, it was necessary to develop a system of government for the first time. The role of a *government* is to **provide the institutions that develop and implement policies for the state**. The state can be a kingdom, a democratic republic, or something in between, but every state needs a government to undertake key tasks and to maintain the functioning of the economic system.

Closely related to the system of government was the **ideological system that justified the existing class structure**. Religions developed that supported the status quo, preaching, for example, the divinity of the Pharaohs and erecting the great pyramids to cement those views. Along with the rise of class interests, we also see the values of the community change. Instead of the solidarity and equality of hunter-gatherer communities, societies divided by classes tended to be much **more individualistic**, with people working more for themselves.

Despite the rise of an unproductive, elite class along with the creation of occupations in government, the army, and the priesthood, the major work of society was still agricultural and done by peasants or slaves. The **peasants** of antiquity did not own their land, which was now owned or controlled by a great lord. But peasants did tend to have rights to farm certain land, and that right was usually passed down to their children. Peasants produced for their own family and handed over a portion of their output (the surplus) to their lord. Peasants produced barely enough food to survive, so they tended to stick with well-known methods and avoid any risky undertaking that could result in starvation. Thus, peasants represented a particular class of people in agricultural systems, with some rights of access to land but with obligations to their lord. Their behavior was governed by **tradition**, including the established social relations, the basic, almost unchanging level of technology, and the **authority** of the lord.

In addition to peasants, the largest ancient human societies relied extensively on slave labor. A **slave** had no control over the resources used to produce goods and services, received only enough food to survive on, and was completely subject to the **authority** of the merchant or lord who owned them. In the city state of ancient Athens in Greece as well as in the Roman Empire, between 30 percent and 80 percent of the people were slaves at various times. Slave economies required large governments and military operations to maintain power and control in the face of regular slave rebellions.

While the peasants and slaves toiled in the rural areas to provide food for society, dynamic but mostly parasitic cities began to develop and grow. In the great cities of ancient Egypt, Greece, or Italy one could find goods in markets from all over the known world. However, most of these goods were luxuries intended for the upper classes and food for the elites and their slaves and servants. The markets of this era fulfilled a limited role compared to their function in modern capitalism. Most of the important resources of society were allocated by tradition or authority (the peasant-lord or slave-owner relationship), while markets supplied a tiny proportion of goods. Furthermore, status (and wealth) was now a product of political, military, or religious power more than one's productivity for the community. With the rise of slavery, productive work came to be denigrated by the elites. Hence, we have the development of the first "leisure class," as Veblen labelled the idle rich of this era, who looked down upon hard agricultural labor and aspired to a life of leisure or non-productive work in warfare, priesthood or government.

Societies of this era did not develop at an equal rate, as Jared Diamond lays out in his book, *Guns, Germs, and Steel*. The groups living in the Middle East, Europe, and Asia had the great luck to have access to the most nutritious grains and the most easily domesticated animals (beasts of burden and animals for food). Greater food production led to higher population densities, and in those densely populated cities people developed resistance to germs. Larger populations also meant more specialization and development of better technology, especially weapons and ships, and more elaborate political and military organizations.

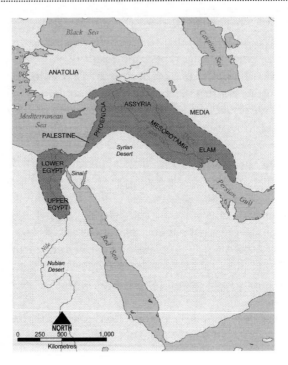

FIGURE 3.1 The Fertile Crescent.

Because of these advantages, the peoples living in the Fertile Crescent area of the Middle East were the first to develop large states, making this region the "cradle of civilization." A series of large empires developed in and around the Fertile Crescent (see Figure 3.1), beginning with Mesopotamia around 2300 BCE, Egypt around 1500 BCE, the Hittites around 1300 BCE, the Assyrians around 715 BCE, the Persians in 539 BCE, Alexander in 334 BCE, and eventually Rome from 50 BCE–456 CE. It is worth briefly examining the Roman Empire as an important example of this type of economic system.

3.3 THE ECONOMIC SYSTEM OF THE ROMAN EMPIRE

At the height of the Roman Empire (Figure 3.2), 1 million residents of the city of Rome were supported by 80–100 million subjects. Impressive military power, effective communication, and efficient transportation networks (roads and ships) allowed Rome to control a huge land area and to generate a steady inflow of goods and wealth. Rome was able to demand rents, taxes, tributes, and gifts from citizens and conquered provinces because of

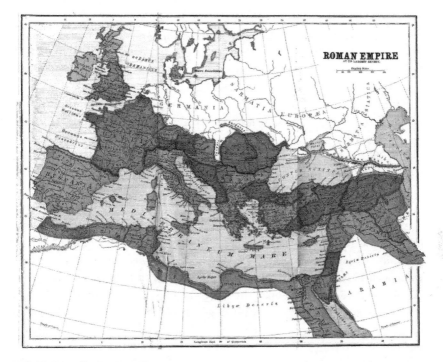

FIGURE 3.2 The Roman Empire.

its military control of the region. Imported products included food (fruits, grains, honey, wine, olive oil, meats), metals (gold and silver to make coins, copper, tin, iron, and lead), materials (marble, ivory, pottery, and cloth), and slaves. These resources were used to maintain the army, administer the government, support the city, and allow the elite to live in luxury.

The class system was complex. The emperor and Roman elite who controlled the Senate, the *patricians*, sat atop the empire and received most of the wealth. They were expected, however, to redistribute some of their wealth to the poor during food shortages and to support public buildings and temples and the army when needed, so some measure of reciprocity still existed. Most professions, including crafts and trading, were considered dishonorable by the elite. Positions were hereditary, with titles and wealth being passed down from fathers to sons. Later, Romans of lower status could become a member of the elite if they amassed enough property.

Underneath the upper class were the freeborn Roman *plebeians*, who varied in rank by wealth and position. Depending on their position, they could be free farmers, merchants, priests, government officials, and craftsmen, or they could be poor peasants and soldiers. They often worked in a variety of occupations alongside freed slaves, who had less rights than plebeians, and non-Roman free people.

Slaves were the largest class of people, and they had no rights. Some of the luckier slaves served the emperor and the elite or worked as craftsmen or teachers, while others toiled in the mines or on farms under brutal conditions. In general, slaves only received subsistence—just enough food, clothing, and shelter to survive—and their surplus production went to their owner.

Although there was growth in many non-agricultural professions, including soldiers, traders, priests, entertainers, and government, 90–95 percent of the population of the Roman Empire was involved in agriculture. In fact, agriculture would continue to dominate the economies of the world until the industrial revolution.

In general, the aristocracy owned and controlled the land and labor of the economy. The emperor controlled trade, shipping, crafts, mines, coinage, tax collection, and markets via a centralized administration housed in Rome. Markets were quite limited, since most goods were produced by peasants or slaves for their master and because transport costs of the time were prohibitive. Also, most of the population consisted of slaves and other people with very little money, limiting the extent of the market. Hence, trade was mostly restricted to luxury goods for the elite, along with goods needed by the military and the state. The government, funded by taxes as well as funds from the emperor and the aristocracy, subsidized grain to reduce civil strife and economic hardship. So Rome had an early version of a welfare state—state support for the least-well-off members of society—to limit the negative consequences of poverty.

Not only were class relations vastly different in the Roman Empire when compared to traditional economies, but there were substantial gender differences as well. By the time of the Roman Empire, women had gone from being roughly equal to men in hunter-gatherer societies to being in a subordinate position. This accompanied the rise in the importance of warriors, and the allocation of captured slaves to those warriors. Men came to dominate farming, using their slaves to do the farm work for them. Cultural attitudes shifted along with these changing roles, until the belief that women were inferior to men became widespread. Women did not have the same rights and privileges as men in Rome; although, they were generally considered to have the same social status as their husbands. The importance of male inheritance of property led to greater restrictions on the sexual behavior of women, as men sought to ensure that their spouses were faithful and bore their children. Men, however, bore no such sexual restrictions and frequently took advantage of their slaves.

Eventually Rome began to stagnate as its slave-based economy became less productive and as the power of the army declined. Slavery was initially very productive as free farmers developed new farming techniques (especially irrigation) and brought new land into cultivation using slave labor.

However, over time, economic growth stagnated. Free farmers, who were driven to increase their status by increasing their wealth, were displaced by the vast slave estates of the elite. The elite looked down on work and technology, and made no effort to develop new farming techniques. Slaves themselves had little interest in innovation because they had to work end-lessly, no matter how innovative they were. Slaves also required intensive supervision and could not be trusted with complex independent tasks or tools that could be used as weapons. Also, the Roman Empire began to run short of slaves because so many died young or were killed (in revolts or in sport), and because of a reduction in conquests as the army's power decreased. The army shrank as the supply of free farmers and peasants dwindled due to war and economic stagnation. After many years of decline Rome fell in 456 CE to Germanic invaders and the era of empires in the Fertile Crescent came to an end. What followed in Europe was the era of feudalism, which lasted for the next 1000 years.

3.4 FEUDALISM AND THE MANOR ECONOMY IN WESTERN EUROPE

Once the Roman Empire collapsed, chaos spread across Europe and the Middle East. Trade routes became dangerous and lawless, and the great cities of the empire could no longer gain access to the goods they needed to survive. Cities shrank, knowledge and expertise were lost, and societies turned inwards.

Amidst the chaos, security and survival became the highest priority. In response, the Roman elite, and later the chiefs of Germanic tribes and other European leaders, turned to a new economic system: Feudalism. Feudalism was organized around independent **manors**, which consisted of large tracts of land (often thousands of acres) controlled by a lord. Slaves were granted greater freedom and became serfs. **Serfs** were obligated to work for their lord on his land a certain number of days each year, in exchange for protection and the right to farm a small amount of land for themselves using the lord's tools (ploughs) and draft animals (oxen and horses). Serfs also had access to common lands where they could farm, graze animals, and collect wood. Thus, there was a degree of reciprocity to the relationship between serfs and lords, even though the relations were highly slanted in favor of the lord.

The serf system was more productive and sustainable than slavery. Serfs had more of an incentive than slaves to work hard for the lord thanks to the protection, stability, and small quantity of property and independ-ence they were granted. Serfs did not need to be supervised the way slaves did, they had little interest in revolting, and they even had an interest in fighting for their lord to protect their own land and house from invaders.

Eventually, all of western Europe came to be divided into independent, self-sufficient, isolated manors. On the manor, the lord was the master of all who lived there, serving as judge, general, and governor. Serfs were tied to the land and to the lord, but they had a measure of security because they could not be removed from their land or their family. The most powerful lords gained control over the most land, becoming kings and demanding loyalty and military support from lesser lords. However, the kings of the feudal era were not very powerful, and most of the wealth and control of the economy rested with the lords.

Like the agriculture-based empires of the Fertile Crescent, feudalism was a system in which resources were allocated by **authority** and **tradition**. The authority of the feudal lord was paramount, and one's station in life was determined traditionally by one's birth. The eldest son of the lord became the next lord. The son of a serf was also a serf. The son of a blacksmith would also become a blacksmith. Serf women worked for lords as servants or makers of clothing, and at home they prepared food, raised the children, and maintained the household. Many serf women were sexually exploited by their lords, however, and women could not own property, so women still occupied an inferior position in society.

Since most feudal manors were self-sufficient, there was very little trade other than a few luxury goods for the lords. However, there were small cities which depended on trade and which hosted traveling fairs of merchants and entertainers, so a small amount commerce did occur in exchange for money.

The towns did have some tradespeople, such as armorers, blacksmiths, shipwrights, potters, weavers, and dyers, indicating that some specialization of labor did exist. But anyone who wanted to produce and sell such goods and services had to join a guild. Guilds were a type of union governing a particular trade or profession. Independent manufacturers, known as guild masters, banded together to set quality standards and wages, limit competition by dividing up territory, and establish rules and codes of conduct. Working for the guild masters were apprentices (usually children of ages 10–12) and adult journeymen who someday hoped to be guild masters.

The guilds were incredibly detailed in the prescriptions governing their members. Rules could include prohibitions on indecent language, the number of threads in a fabric, the type of equipment to be used in construction, how a particular task was to be completed, etc. Traditional methods of production were passed down through the guilds, and innovation was strongly discouraged. A new product or new process for making a product had to be approved by the guild, but such innovations were usually rejected as a threat to other producers. If one craftsman developed a superior technique, it might displace other craftsmen and upset the accepted order of things. In a society that prized safety and stability above all else, this was unacceptable, so any deviation from approved procedures often resulted in imprisonment, torture, or even death! The emphasis was clearly on maintaining the status quo and resisting change. Unsurprisingly, given that the utilization of new techniques could lead to dire outcomes, very little innovation occurred during the feudalist era. Over these 1000 years, there were only a handful of major innovations—clocks, the blast furnace, eyeglasses, the spinning wheel, and the printing press being among the most important.

In this system of decentralized manors, the Catholic Church was the largest owner of land. As a result, the Catholic religion played a huge role in shaping society and its values. A tour of the cathedrals of Europe built during the feudal era demonstrates that, of the little surplus that was produced, the majority went to the church. In addition, religious prescriptions played a prominent role in the economy. For example, merchants were expected to charge a "just price," selling items for what they were worth and no more. Greed was considered to be a sin, a corrupting influence to be scorned and even punished. The notion of profit or personal gain was largely condemned until very recently in human history.

In fact, money-lending was considered to be so sinful under Catholicism that moneylenders were to be excommunicated from the church. The prohibition against moneylending was grounded in the New Testament of the Bible, which condemned usury. However, the Old Testament of the Bible allowed Jews to lend to non-Jews. As a result, many European Jews, barred from most professions by guilds and prohibited from owning land, turned to moneylending to Christians in order to make a living. The Jewish monopoly on moneylending meant that they could make a lot of money, but Christians resented the success of Jewish moneylenders based on biblical condemnations of usury. There was much Christian hostility toward Jews stemming from this strained relationship. As an example, the entire community of 150 Jews of York, England was killed in 1190 due to religious intolerance and the anger of those who were indebted to them. The roots of much anti-Semitism in Europe can be traced to the feudal era and the differing views of Christians and Jews on the acceptability of money-lending.

The characteristics of feudal society help us to understand why life in Europe went largely unchanged for 1000 years. The small amount of surplus that was produced went to provide military protection or was squandered on luxuries for the lords and the church. Without any substantial investment, and with substantial resistance to technological change, there was very little economic growth. However, over time, a series of changes undermined Feudalism, stimulated the rise of markets, and reshaped European societies.

3.5 THE FORCES BEHIND THE DECLINE OF FEUDALISM AND THE RISE OF MARKETS

The major changes that eroded the institutions of feudalism and created the conditions for the development of markets were changes in technology, urbanization and specialization, increased long-distance trade, the Crusades, the establishment of the nation-state, exploration and colonization, the rise of Protestantism, the development of early manufacturing and factories, the monetization of the economy, and the establishment of private property rights. The section below describes these changes and how they moved the feudal economies of Europe toward the market capitalist system of mercantilism. One crucial change that prompted many of the other changes was the increase in the surplus of food that occurred when better agricultural technology was developed.

1. An increase in the surplus from improvements in agricultural technology

In an agriculturally based economy, agricultural technology is the primary determinant of the amount of surplus a community has. Yearly planting of the same crops in the same soil eventually depletes the land and can even render the land unusable. To avoid this problem, farmers had developed a system where land would be used to grow crops one year, but then it would lie fallow (unused) the next year to allow the soil to recover. Eventually, around the year 1000, a 3-field crop rotation system was developed. A grain (rye or winter wheat) would be planted in 1 field in the fall, a second crop (peas, oats, or beans) would be planted in a second field in the spring and a third field would lie fallow. Rotating crops between these 3 uses improved the health of the soil, and the land only had to lie fallow one-third of the time instead of half of the time. Productivity increased significantly, generating additional food that could support more people and surplus grains that could support more horses and other farm animals. Horses not only made farming more productive, but they could be used to transport goods for trade. With the rise in food production, Europe's population doubled between 1000 and 1300, and, as a consequence, there was a significant increase in urbanization.

2. Urbanization and specialization

The towns of Europe began to grow steadily as food supplies increased. Since they existed outside of the influence of the feudal lords, who controlled rural areas but not the towns, the urban areas were forced to develop their own codes of law, monetary system, and governing institutions. For their survival they depended on local trade, which meant that they needed to produce specialized goods that the rural areas needed and would buy in exchange for food. Greater surpluses and better transportation made trade easier, encouraging still more specialization and exchange. Local trade grew steadily, but it was carefully regulated by town officials to preserve stability, especially jobs, incomes, and food supplies. Long distance trade, on the other hand, was the province of international traveling merchants and was not subject to the same regulation.

3. Long distance trade and traveling merchants

Traveling merchants became more prominent from 700–1300. Originally, they traded spices, salted fish, wine, and goods that were only produced in certain places (dyes, special cloth, fine metalwork, etc.). As trade routes became more established (around the 1400s), permanent markets featuring goods from distant lands became a feature of towns. Regions of Europe began to specialize increasingly in the production of specific types of goods, which led to improvements in skill and productivity, resulting in even more surplus to trade. Great trading cities developed to facilitate long-distance trade, and they created legal and banking systems for businesses that formed the basis for modern market capitalist systems. Further facilitating this trade was the Crusades.

4. The Crusades and the opening of Europe

From 1095–1291, hundreds of thousands of European knights and peasants traveled to the Middle East at the behest of the Catholic Church to protect Catholic interests and free the holy lands from non-Catholics. The Crusades were only somewhat successful militarily, and the crusading soldiers were often manipulated by the commercial interests of Venice into attacking Venetian rivals instead of their intended targets. But the major long-term effect of the Crusades was economic: Sheltered Europeans came in contact with the thriving, dynamic commercial societies of Venice and Byzantium. They were impressed by the opulent lifestyle, and they returned to Europe with spices, exotic trinkets, and tales of luxury that could be obtained by trade. Europe began to look increasingly outward. But this outward orientation required different political arrangements.

5. The rise of the nation-state and commercial interests

Trade under feudalism was a complicated affair. Every time a merchant set foot on the land of an estate or a town, he would have to pay a tax or duty of some sort. Along the German section of the Rhine in 1400, there were more than 60 toll stations! It was not uncommon for tolls to double the prices of goods as they were hauled by merchants from where they were produced to where they were sold. As trade increased in importance, merchants chafed under the stifling commercial system of feudalism. They found an ally in the kings who were looking to expand their influence over the largely independent feudal lords. Kings, with the financial support of merchants, began to expand their power and influence and develop larger and larger kingdoms. They amassed armies and built navies using the revenues from trade, stimulating manufacturing in the process. By the 1500s, Europe was a collection of nation-states with growing economic and military power under the control of kings and merchants. Kings and merchants relied on trade to generate gold and silver, which were needed for hiring mercenaries and maintaining an army and navy. Because money meant the ability to purchase military power (gold meant power), they worked incessantly to increase trade and the supply of gold as much as possible. One of the ways that they could do this was by finding new places to trade with and new sources of raw materials and gold.

6. Exploration and colonization by nation-states

While some exploration did occur during feudalism, it took the concentrated power and wealth of the new kings of Europe to undertake large scale exploration. Kings outfitted fleets for exploration under the direction of the likes of Vasco Da Gama (Portugal), Christopher Columbus (Spain), John Cabot (England), Jacques Cartier (France), and Oliver van Noort (the Netherlands). In addition to exotic goods and trade routes, explorers sought gold, silver, and slaves to pay off the high costs of these ventures and to support the kings who financed them.

Christopher Columbus's log describing his landing in the Bahamas, quoted in Howard Zinn's book, *A People's History of the United States*, illustrates the attitudes of the merchants and explorers of the newfound nation-states of Europe:

> [The Arawaks] brought us parrots and balls of cotton and spears and many other things, which they exchanged for the glass beads and hawks' bells. They willingly traded everything they owned... They were well-built, with good bodies and handsome features... They do not bear arms, and do not know them, for I showed them a sword, they took it by the edge and cut themselves out of ignorance. They have no iron. Their spears are made of cane... They would make fine servants... With fifty men we could subjugate them all and make them do whatever we want.

Europe's advanced weaponry and resistance to disease, a product of a longer history of close-quarters living, allowed them to dominate and decimate large areas of the earth as they roamed the planet in search of riches. Eventually, the European countries established colonial empires in the Americas, Africa, and Asia designed to funnel resources and gold to Europe, often using slave labor. This was trade of a particularly exploitative sort, but it served to stimulate Europe tremendously and transform it into a vibrant commercial center. In the process, greed had displaced the feudal prohibitions on such behavior, marking a major shift in ideology and religion.

7. The rise of Protestantism, individualism, and greed

Following close on the heels of the first wave of exploration was the development of Calvinism, the first Protestant religion, in the 1500s. The Catholic Church of the feudal era was primarily concerned with the after-life, and it explicitly condemned any obsession with the accumulation of worldly possessions and any form of greed. Also, the church was supposed to be the primary focus of the community, not the individual. Individuals were supposed to know their place in society and work to maintain their station in life, not to change it.

Calvinists, in contrast, saw hard work and professional activity as one's calling and a sign of godliness. Individual wealth accumulation from hard work was actually considered to be evidence of doing God's work. Additionally, wealth was to be invested in further productive endeavors rather than wasted on luxuries. Even earning income from interest on loans was acceptable as a sign of engaging in a productive, profitable venture.

In many ways, Calvinism and later variations of Protestantism pro-vided the ideal ideological support for a market capitalist economic sys-tem based on self-interest, greed, hard work, and reinvestment. The idea of improving one's standing in society and celebrating the riches earned through hard work helped foster economic growth. Not surprisingly, it was the nations in which Protestantism took the greatest hold that developed the earliest and most robust market systems. England, in par-ticular, had the strongest departure from Catholicism and embracing of Protestantism when King Henry VIII and the Church of England broke with the papacy in the 1530s. Meanwhile, the earliest forms of capitalist manufacturing were also getting started.

8. The putting-out system and the beginnings of capitalist factories

As markets expanded rapidly in the 1500s, merchants operating in export industries needed a larger and more reliable supply of goods to sell. Instead of relying on small, independent craftsmen to produce goods for them, they started the **putting-out system**. The merchant provided the craftsman with the materials, the craftsman worked the materials into finished products using their tools and skills, and the merchant collected and sold the finished products. Merchants eventually began to set up entire buildings with tools and equipment and hired journeymen and apprentices with the requisite skills, bypassing independent craftsmen entirely. These were the first capitalist factories. Independent craftsmen were gradually replaced by larger-scale factories and workers, breaking down the guilds that had governed production, and turning independent craftsmen into laborers who worked for a merchant-capitalist. Merchant-capitalists began developing markets for buying and selling inputs, including labor, to use in their new factories. Consider, for a moment, how revolutionary this was. In prior human history, labor had always been allocated based on a social relationship governed by tradition or authority. Now, labor was starting to be allocated to the highest bidder. For the first time in human history, labor and significant amounts of resources were allocated based on money in markets and not by tradition or authority.

9. The monetization of the economy and the decline of the manor

The growing urban populations of Europe needed increasing amounts of food, which they paid for with money earned from manufacturing and trading. Meanwhile, the rural lords wanted additional money to buy all of the new goods that were becoming available. As a result, lords began switching from demanding payments from serfs in fixed amounts of goods (in-kind payments) to demanding payments in fixed amounts of money. Ironically, this set the stage for the economic decline of the manor. As gold from the new world flooded Europe, prices began to rise dramatically. From 1520 –1650, prices in Europe increased by between 150 and 400 percent. Lords found that their fixed payments from serfs bought less and less goods, and many became impoverished.

These trends were exacerbated by a significant decline in the population from the Black Death of the 1300s and the Hundred Years' War between England and France (1337–1453). These events wiped out almost 40 percent of England's population and led to a labor shortage there and elsewhere in Europe. Without enough labor, lords attempted to squeeze the remaining serfs to generate enough money to support the manor. The serfs responded with a series of revolts. The result of the serf resistance—combined with the competition between lords for the labor services of the serfs—led many serfs to gain the status of independent, free peasants with the right to farm their traditional plot as well as the common lands. This put the rural lords in a desperate situation. Their only recourse was to seize as much land as possible to generate cash to support the manor.

10. The enclosure movement and the establishment of private property rights

To generate cash income, lords began seizing the common lands for their own use. In England, lords fenced off (enclosed) common lands in order to raise sheep for the booming textile industry. Similar patterns followed in continental Europe as lords seized common lands to raise animals or crops that could be sold for cash. By the 1700s, 75–90 percent of peasants had been forced off of farms all over Europe and into urban slums. This, coupled with a rising population and rising rural rents, meant that cities had huge, desperate populations of former peasants with no means of subsistence. They had no land or tools, and only their labor power to sell.

At the same time, the enclosure movement established the legal right of lords to the land they seized. The lords began to use the land as productively as possible to generate the income they needed, and the use of land came to be associated with the amount or revenue or rent that it could bring. Lands were sometimes rented out to others in exchange for money since money was of higher value to lords than produced goods.

Thus, the enclosure movement had the doubly important impact of creating a market for labor power (former serfs and peasants who had to sell their labor in order to survive) and a market for land (which now could be sold or rented). Labor and land had become commodities to be bought and sold. This is a far cry from traditional feudal relationships in which labor was a social obligation and land was a family's estate or plot, both established by birth.

We also see how private property can be both constructive and destructive. If a property owner is secure in their ownership of the land for the foreseeable future, they are willing to invest in the productivity of the land by adding irrigation, breeding draft animals, fertilizing, and so on. On the other hand, privatizing the common lands cast millions of peasants into desperate, landless poverty.

The culmination of all of these changes in the feudal era was the establishment of the first market-based economic system, mercantilism. By the late 1500s and early 1600s, most of the major cities of England, France, Spain, Belgium, and Holland were incorporated into countries that were dominated by huge merchant-capitalists and the monarchs who were allied with them. These merchant-capitalists controlled almost all trade and manufacturing.

3.6 MERCANTILISM AND THE UNEASY BEGINNINGS OF CAPITALISM

National, market-based economic systems did not evolve naturally during mercantilism. They were created by the merchant-capitalists and monarchs of Europe for their benefit. A national market system was resisted vigorously by the smaller towns and rural areas, which fought to maintain their tight regulation of local trade and preserve existing jobs. As Polanyi noted in *The Great Transformation*, "The towns raised every possible obstacle to the formation of a national or internal market for which the capitalist wholesaler was pressing." It took deliberate actions by the state in the 1400s and 1500s to break down the fiercely protectionist policies of the towns. Once local resistance was broken, the state replaced local rules on trading and manufacturing with national rules, so mercantilism was not free-wheeling, competitive market capitalism. It was tightly controlled national capitalism run by and for the merchant-capitalists and monarchs, grounded in the social hierarchies of the period.

The early mercantilist countries tried to maximize the inflow of gold, an approach known as **bullionism**, to cement their power and wealth. To do this, they tried to maintain a trade surplus by subsidizing and encouraging exports while taxing and discouraging imports. One of the best ways to do this was to grant companies trading monopolies in specific areas of the market. If only one British merchant was allowed to purchase red dye from France, he could buy it more cheaply than if multiple British merchants were bidding for the same dye. If only one British merchant was allowed to sell red cloth in England, that merchant could sell it for the highest possible price. Trading was carefully regulated so that the system maximized the profits of the monopoly merchant-capitalists and insured an inflow of gold.

Colonial empires also improved profits from trading. Resources, especially raw materials and slave labor, could be had cheaply from the colonies. The British dismantled the thriving textile industry in India and forced the colony to export raw cotton to England, where it could be used by British industries to manufacture textiles. Similar practices occurred in Africa, Asia, and the Americas, as industries in the colonies were displaced in favor of the production of raw materials for export to the colonial power.

The Transatlantic Slave Trade was a particularly horrific example of mercantilist trading patterns. Slave ships left England for West Africa carrying cloth, guns, alcohol, iron wares, and other manufactured goods. These were traded in West Africa for slaves who were captured by African chiefs collaborating with the English traders. The ships then traveled to the West Indies in the Caribbean (and later the United States) where the slaves were sold at auctions to plantation owners. The ships were then loaded with the produce from the plantations, especially commodities like sugar, coffee, tobacco, and cotton, which were brought back to England. Merchants profited from each stage of the trade, while extracting resources from Africa and the Americas.

In some cases, private companies such as the Dutch East India Company were put in charge of vast colonial territories and granted the power to wage war, mete out justice, execute convicts, establish new colonies, mint coins, and so on. They exploited colonial territories ruthlessly for their own profit. Imagine how the most racist and rapacious company without any check on its behavior might exploit a country in Africa, Asia, or the Americas for its own benefit, and you will get some idea of the horrors of mercantilism.

Initially, countries experienced economic growth under tightly controlled mercantilism. The expansion of markets internally within the countries and externally to their colonies enhanced profits and stimulated the development of new industries. But the control of the economy by the monarch and a handful of huge firms began to stifle the development of new firms and industries. Stimulated by the growth of trade, an emerging group of capitalists working in mining, manufacturing, and other industries chafed at the restricted, monopolized markets. They wanted more trade, greater access to domestic and foreign markets, and fewer government restrictions on their behavior. At the same time, mercantilism experienced some major economic problems: The enclosure of the common lands had created large pools of desperately poor workers without sufficient jobs or opportunities, and fluctuations in the supply of gold caused large swings in prices. Such a system, which worked well only for a small part of the population, ultimately proved to be unstable.

Just as the mercantilist economy was becoming more and more untenable, Adam Smith offered a vision of how capitalism could solve the problems created under mercantilism. His vision of a lightly regulated market capitalist economy proved to be very attractive to the increasingly powerful capitalists of England in the late 1700s and early 1800s. By 1834, England had abandoned mercantilism and embarked on an experiment in market capitalism that would reshape the entire world. This is the subject of the next chapter.

3.7 CONCLUSION

As we have seen, the economic systems of human societies have taken a wide variety of forms. The traditional economies of hunter-gatherer societies were small, egalitarian, self-sufficient, redistributive, and cooperative.

The slave empires of Rome and the Fertile Crescent were large, hierarchical and exploitative, with a small volume of trade primarily for the elites. The feudal manors of Europe were small, self-sufficient, and hierarchical, with less trade than the Roman Empire. Finally, the mercantilist countries of Europe were large, profit- and trade-oriented, and monopolistic. Tradition and authority were the main methods by which resources were allocated under all human societies until mercantilism in Europe, when markets came to dominate the economic system for the first time. But even under mercantilism, the social structure of society, especially which class a person was born into, was crucial in determining who had access to resources and who did not. The specialization of labor and the generation and use of the surplus product were important features of all human societies, determining whether an economy experienced growth or stagnation. Stagnation, and other intractable contradictions, tended to result in the elimination of one type of economic system and the gradual development of another.

Stagnation and the pressures from the new capitalist class provoked changes in the mercantilist economic system. First in England, and then around Europe, one country after another switched from mercantilism to lightly regulated market capitalism. The next chapter turns to the fall of mercantilism, the rise of capitalism, and the ideas of Adam Smith, who provided a powerful intellectual argument in favor of a capitalist economic system.

QUESTIONS FOR REVIEW

1. What factors determined who did what job (how labor was allocated) in (a) traditional, hunter-gatherer societies, (b) slave-based empires such as Rome, (c) feudalism, and (d) mercantilism?
2. Why do political economists think that human beings are inherently social beings with strong levels of group identity? Is there evidence from economic history to support this view? Why or why not?
3. Describe the role played by (a) tradition, (b) authority, and (c) markets in traditional, slave, feudal, and mercantilist economic systems.
4. How did the role and status of women change as economic systems evolved from traditional economies to mercantilism?
5. Why is the specialization of labor important to understanding historical economic development?
6. How is the generation and utilization of the surplus product important to understanding economic development?

7. Construct an argument agreeing or disagreeing with the following statement: *All human societies involve a large degree of cooperation, redistribution and reciprocity.* Use specific examples to support your argument.

8. List the main social classes in each of the following economic systems: (a) Traditional (hunter-gatherer), (b) the Roman Empire, (c) feudalism, and (d) mercantilism.

9. Describe how social classes evolved from traditional economies through mercantilism. How did the determination of status (which people were held in highest esteem) change?

10. How has the role of private property changed as economic systems evolved?

11. How did attitudes toward greed change as economic systems evolved?

12. List and analyze the major forces that eroded each economic system and paved the way for the next economic system.

13. Construct an argument for which 2 factors were most important in eroding feudalism and paving the way for mercantilism. Use specific examples to support your argument.

Adam Smith and the rise of capitalism

The era of laissez-faire

As the problems of mercantilism began to mount, a dynamic new economic system began to develop in England. A group of early entrepreneurs was able to make large sums of money manufacturing textiles and a few other goods using new technologies they developed. They reinvested their profits in new ventures, spurring rapid economic growth.

Adam Smith saw the earliest stages of capitalism occurring around him and realized the tremendous potential of the system. Smith believed that lightly regulated capitalism would be preferable to mercantilism, a system where the king and a select group of monopolistic merchants dominated the economy for their own benefit. Smith hoped that a capitalist system, with sufficient competition to keep businesses innovative and efficient, would result in greater productivity and lower prices for goods. This would, in theory, result in a higher standard of living for all people as the number of jobs increased and the prices of necessities decreased. Thus, Smith hoped that capitalism would solve the major problem that mercantilism had been unable to fix: The vast amount of poverty created by the enclosure movement. Smith and some other pro-market economists, along with their allies among the capitalist class, were able to push England to adopt the world's first capitalist economic system.

This chapter describes the roots of capitalism in England. We then take up Adam Smith's ideas regarding how he thought capitalism would work, and why he thought it was preferable to mercantilism. Next, the chapter describes the triumph of laissez-faire ideas in the debates over the Poor Laws, macroeconomic crises, and restrictions on trade. By the mid-1800s, England had eliminated most of its mercantilist regulations and embarked on a radical experiment in laissez-faire capitalism.

4.0 CHAPTER 4 LEARNING GOALS

After reading this chapter you should be able to:

- List and analyze the key institutions that supported the establishment of capitalism in England;
- Describe the major economic concepts in Smith's critique of mercantilism;
- Identify the major components of Smith's analysis of capitalism, and critically evaluate which of his ideas still hold true when applied to modern capitalism;
- Explain and critically assess the arguments of laissez-faire economists against English Poor Laws, macroeconomic intervention, and trade protectionism; and,
- Define Karl Polanyi's concept of the double movement, and apply this concept to the modern world.

We begin by considering what differentiates capitalism from other economic systems, and the institutional factors that provided the foundation for capitalism in England in the 1700s.

4.1 THE INDUSTRIAL REVOLUTION AND CAPITALISM IN ENGLAND

Hunter-gatherer societies revolved around using labor to generate enough food to survive. The invention of agriculture spawned the empires and later the feudal system. These economies relied on agricultural production and the exploitation of slave and peasant labor by the elites, who seized any available surpluses for themselves. During the era of mercantilism, the importance of trade and commerce came to the fore—although the wealth of mercantilist economies was still primarily based on agricultural output from slave and peasant labor. Thus, human economies from the beginning of time revolved around labor and agriculture.

The industrial revolution changed everything. The creation of the industrial factory signaled the rise in importance of **capital,** machinery, equipment, buildings, and other technological resources used to produce factory goods. First in England, then across Europe and around the globe, the Industrial Revolution made ownership of capital the major source of economic power and the foremost driver of change in the economy. *Capitalism* **is an economic system in which the capital goods and other productive resources (land, natural resources) are privately owned and are bought and**

sold in markets based on the pursuit of profits. Under a capitalist economic system, workers, instead of laboring for themselves and keeping the proceeds, sell their labor power to the capitalist in exchange for wages. The capitalist, as the owner, gets to keep any surplus that is produced.

Under capitalism, the primary focus of all economic activity is profit. An owner takes a large sum of money and invests it in setting up a factory and hiring workers. Those workers produce a commodity of some kind. That commodity is (hopefully) sold for a greater value than the initial investment.

$$\text{Money}(M) \rightarrow \text{Commodities}(C) \rightarrow \text{More Money}(M')$$

Early entrepreneurs had to advance a considerable sum of money ahead of time to cover costs, with no assurance that they would get a substantial return once a commodity was produced. This uncertain situation made them, as described by economic historian Paul Mantoux, "tyrannical, hard, sometimes cruel."

The Industrial Revolution began around 1760 in England with just such a group of "hard" entrepreneurs. The reasons for the Industrial Revolution's conception in England, as opposed to elsewhere, are important because they help us understand the key institutions that provide the basis for a capitalist economic system.

First, England was **ideologically** better suited toward a money-oriented, invention-driven capitalist economy. As the heart of the Protestant reformation, English society was less opposed to the notion of making money. As a result, members of the English aristocracy were early supporters of commerce and manufacturing, and businessmen who made a lot of money were accepted into high society much more readily than elsewhere in Europe. This "worldly" attitude also carried over into an interest in science and engineering. The Royal Society was founded in London in 1660 to promote "natural knowledge" and establish principles of scientific inquiry and experimentation. England became the international scientific leader, which led to a host of discoveries and inventions. The establishment of a national patent system to protect the rights of inventors to the profits from their discoveries further spurred technological change.

Second, England was the site of the most comprehensive enclosure movement and, consequently, the most complete elimination of feudal society, which resulted in the most secure system of **property rights.** The interest of the English aristocracy in exporting wool to obtain gold and foreign luxuries made it particularly aggressive in seizing the common lands from the peasants. Thus, the privatization of land and the creation of a vast quantity of **landless laborers** were more prevalent in England than elsewhere. A factory owner could only start an industrial operation if the inputs he needed were available: He needed laborers who were willing and able to work for reasonable wages and land that could be rented or purchased for the site of his factory. Both of these conditions were present in England.

Third, England was wealthy, and this created a **large market** for manufactured products. Manufacturing large quantities of goods in a factory is only profitable if there is a sizable market for those goods. There must be enough people with ample income to create sufficient demand for large quantities of products. England's vast colonial empire, rigged to generate profits from slave trading, piracy, colonial commerce, and more, created a relatively large (for that time) upper-middle class and a very rich upper class. These groups were only too happy to consume the latest manufactured goods. The colonies also served as suppliers of cheap raw materials, and as market outlets for English manufactured goods. The extensive colonial trade of England also included a well-developed transportation system which made trade in manufactured goods relatively easy and low-cost. Also, England was lucky to have large deposits of coal and iron ore, which were crucial in early manufacturing. Luck, alongside the vast colonial empire, meant plenty of **cheap inputs** and **captive markets** for English manufacturers. The result was a system in which immense profits could be earned if entrepreneurs were willing to invest sufficient sums of money. Many were willing to do so, and their successes encouraged other entrepreneurs to follow.

With cheap labor and inputs available to purchase, land available to rent, profits to invest, and an ideological approach favoring the acquisition of money, the way was paved for the rise of capitalism. In the process, there was a fundamental shift from labor and land as a part of social and cultural relations to labor and land as commodities to be bought and sold.

In such a system, the owners of capital had the greatest amount of power in society. Landowners needed rent from their land in order to generate income. The best way to generate income from the land was to rent to a capitalist, who would use the land to its greatest capacity. The best way for a laborer to earn a living was to work for a capitalist. Given that there were many more people looking for work than there were jobs, the capitalist employer had a huge advantage in the relationship with workers. Most workers of the time had to take whatever wage rate the employer offered and accept work even in oppressive conditions since the alternative was starvation. As British economist Joan Robinson observed in her book, *Economic Philosophy*, "The misery of being exploited by capitalists is nothing compared to the misery of not being exploited at all." Meanwhile, the capitalists, who had to advance a considerable amount of money without the guarantee of a return on their investment, worked to drive very hard bargains with workers and land owners. Thus, with the rise of capitalism in the mid-1700s, we see for the first time in human history the notion of individual gain—the profit motive—becoming an all-pervasive force in society, driving the behavior of workers, landowners, and capitalists.

There was deep unease in England as capitalism was stirring. The mercantilist system was not able to solve the major problems of society, especially the massive amount of poverty. The early capitalist enterprises were very promising, but their expansion was limited by the strict regulations on trade put into place to benefit the monopolistic merchants. Into this environment stepped Adam Smith, who is usually credited with inventing the field of economics, and who argued that a lightly regulated market capitalist economic system would solve the problems of mercantilism.

4.2 ADAM SMITH, LAISSEZ-FAIRE CAPITALISM, AND SMITH'S CRITIQUE OF MERCANTILISM

In the budding capitalism occurring around him, Smith saw the possibilities for an economic system that he hoped could solve the major problems of mercantilism. That system was limited laissez-faire (lightly regulated) capitalism. Laissez-faire is French for "let it be." When applied to the economy, a laissez-faire approach means letting the market run without significant interference from the government.

Adam Smith (1723–1790), pictured in Figure 4.1, lived most of his life in Scotland, where he was surrounded by dynamic entrepreneurs such as his friend, James Watt. Watt invented a revolutionary steam engine that was an essential part of the Industrial Revolution.

These entrepreneurs needed access to new markets for inputs and goods so that they could produce on a larger scale. The only way to recoup the large investment needed to set up a factory was to get inputs at low prices and to sell large quantities of the product that the factory was producing. But mercantilist monopolies dominated trade, charging high prices for the commodities that entrepreneurs needed as inputs and limiting entrepreneurs' access to foreign markets. Smith argued that mercantilist policies were limiting economic growth and preventing the alleviation of poverty for 3 main reasons.

First, with every European country strictly regulating trade and preventing imports of manufactured goods, manufacturing firms could only produce for the domestic market. With free trade, firms would be able to sell their products to multiple countries, and that would allow them to produce more goods on a larger scale, which would be more efficient.

FIGURE 4.1 Adam Smith.

Factories could be larger, which would promote the development of additional machinery and workers with more specialized skills. Below, we will go into more detail about the importance of specialization.

Second, mercantilist policies reduced competition, allowing monopolies to form in key sectors. Without competition, monopolistic firms did not have to be efficient or innovative to make a profit. Thus, the creation of monopolistic markets was a major barrier to development, keeping prices high and growth low.

Third, Smith objected to mercantilist policies to suppress wages. These policies encouraged employers in a particular trade or geographical area to form a trade association, which could then meet to set wages at the lowest possible level. If employers were instead forced to compete with each other for workers, they would tend to bid up wages in seeking to lure the best people from other firms. Agreeing to a fixed wage rate for the area eliminated such competition and kept wages low.

In Smith's view, the 2 great evils of his era were the **government** and the **monopolies** that set up the mercantilist system for their own benefit. The way to solve the poverty problem was, he thought, to stop the government from interfering with markets and to let competition force firms to be efficient and innovative. This, he hoped, would raise the standard of living of all citizens, especially the poor.

4.3 SMITH'S IDEALIZED PICTURE OF A CAPITALIST SYSTEM

Smith believed that lightly regulated capitalism was preferable to mercantilism based on how he envisioned a competitive market capitalist system working. The key difference between this system and mercantilism would be its effect on economic growth. Smith's economics book was titled *The Wealth of Nations* in large part because he sought to analyze the determinants of wealth.

Smith's first important insight was that **wealth comes from productivity,** not from money (gold). Money is only useful if it can lead to a high standard of living, but a country's standard of living is determined by how productive it is—how many goods and services it can produce and consume—not how much money it has. A country that has lots of gold but produces very few goods will quickly find that the prices of those few goods are very high. But a country that is very productive will be able to consume lots of goods and services, no matter how much money it has. The fact that countries today use gross domestic product, which is the total production of goods and services in an economy, to measure the standard of living of people in an economy is a testament to Smith's enduring insight.

Second, Smith identified **the importance of the specialization of labor in enhancing productivity** (and wealth). As noted before, the specialization of labor occurs when particular tasks are performed by specific individuals, rather than everyone performing all tasks. This enhances productivity for 3 reasons, according to Smith. First, workers get better at their job, improving their skill and dexterity, when they specialize in 1 task instead of many tasks. Second, less time is spent moving from 1 job to another. Third, specialization leads to the invention of machines that facilitate and replace labor. The last of these tends to be the most important driver of increases in productivity.

A good example of the importance of specialization comes from the car industry. The first cars were produced by teams of skilled craftsmen and entrepreneurs. But once entrepreneurs divided the manufacturing process into discrete tasks and developed specialized machinery, the manufacturing process became much more productive. Each car part could be manufactured using a specialized process, which was subdivided into a series of even more specialized tasks. In Figure 4.2, we see workers on the first moving assembly line in 1913 assembling magnetos and flywheels, which was a part of a Ford car.

Another crucial insight in Smith's analysis was the importance of **competition** in making markets work efficiently and fostering growth. In the absence of competition, monopolistic companies could produce shoddy

FIGURE 4.2 The first moving assembly line for 1913 Ford cars.

products and charge high prices because consumers had no other options. These companies also had no incentive to invest in new technology or products since they could continue to make profits indefinitely without fear of new competition. Additionally, they could pay workers very little because other companies were not competing to hire workers. Competition changes all of this. Competitive markets tend to generate better quality, lower prices, more innovations, and higher wages.

Ideally, Smith hoped, **competition would** even **regulate incomes and benefit the poor,** solving the huge poverty problem of the day. Smith envisioned the pattern unfolding as follows: (1) Bold entrepreneurs, trying to get ahead of their competition, engage in risky innovations, such as creating a new product or designing a more cost-effective method of production (technology). (2) If effective, the new product or technology yields substantial economic (above-normal) profits and the business expands. (3) Timid entrepreneurs, once they see that the innovation is effective, copy the new product or imitate the new technology, causing new firms to enter the market to compete with the bold entrepreneur. (4) The entrance of more competition increases the supply of the product, lowering the price and eliminating the excess profits earned by the bold entrepreneur. (5) The industry as a whole experiences economic growth as multiple businesses expand operations as a result of building the new product or utilizing the new technology. (6) This process tends to limit the incomes of the rich via competition and raise the standard of living of the poor because goods' prices are kept low and demand for workers increases as industries expand. The result, according to Smith, is that a much more equal distribution of income would result in this capitalist economic system than was the case under mercantilism!

In highlighting the importance of competition, Smith also identified **self-interest** as a useful component of a market capitalist economy. The dynamic entrepreneurs of his era were providing essential goods and services to society, but they were doing so for selfish reasons—to make a profit: "It is not from the benevolence of the butcher, the brewer, or the baker, that we expect our dinner, but from their regard to their own interest. We address ourselves, not to their humanity but to their self-love, and never talk to them of our own necessities but of their advantages." To Smith, the profit motive, in the presence of sufficient competition, was a positive force providing the essential goods that society wanted and leading to economic growth in the process.

Along with competition, Smith believed that **moral sentiments** and a **system of justice** were key regulators of the competitive process. In his first important book, *The Theory of Moral Sentiments*, Smith states, "How selfish soever man may be supposed, there are evidently some principles in his nature, which interest him in the fortune of others, and render their happiness necessary to him." Smith evidently saw people as both self-interested *and* interested in the welfare of others. Along with moral sentiments, Smith envisioned a government which had "the duty of protecting, as far as possible, every member of the society from the injustice and oppression of every other member of it, or the duty of establishing an exact administration of justice."

Combining these crucial ideas, to Smith, *a self-interested entrepreneur who (a) operates in a competitive market, (b) cares about the welfare of others, and (c) is prevented by law from exploiting others would tend to serve the public interest by producing good products at low prices, innovating regularly, fostering economic growth, and benefitting the poor.* This led Smith to his famous analogy of the **invisible hand** of the market:

> As every individual ... endeavours as much as he can both to employ his capital in the support of domestic industry, and so to direct that industry that its produce may be of the greatest value; every individual necessarily labours to render the annual revenue of the society as great as he can. He generally, indeed, neither intends to promote the public interest, nor knows how much he is promoting it. By preferring the support

of domestic to that of foreign industry, he intends only his own security; and by directing that industry in such a manner as its produce may be of the greatest value, he intends only his own gain, and he is in this, as in many other cases, led by an invisible hand to promote an end which was no part of his intention. Nor is it always the worse for the society that it was no part of it. By pursuing his own interest he frequently promotes that of the society more effectually than when he really intends to promote it.

This was a powerful and counter-intuitive claim. Self-interest, via the competitive market system, can end up benefitting society more effectively than intentionally benevolent acts! Consider this idea carefully and evaluate whether or not you think it holds true in our world.

Given what Smith actually said about capitalism, as described above, it is interesting how many commentators cite the portion of Smith's work on self-interest without acknowledging the other crucial components of the system that Smith discussed. Smith only mentioned the invisible hand once in *The Wealth of Nations,* so selecting this metaphor as the key to understanding Smith's work is questionable.

Smith was also a strong advocate of reducing regulations on imports and exports. He thought that with less regulated trade companies could sell goods to a larger market (foreign as well as domestic consumers). This in turn would allow companies to increase the size of their factories, leading to greater specialization, the development of new machines, and ultimately greater productivity and economic growth. Smith thought that the result would be an improvement in everyone's standard of living as productivity increases resulted in lower prices and greater quantities of goods.

Despite Smith's distrust of government, which in his day acted on behalf of monopolistic interests rather than promoting the public welfare, Smith still saw a limited role for government policy. Smith's approach to government regulation is termed "limited laissez-faire" because he did envision a few limits being placed on market capitalism. First, as noted earlier, Smith wanted the government to establish a strong system of justice to protect every member of society from injustice and oppression. Second, the government needed to maintain order and provide for national defense. Third, the government needed to provide public goods, including roads, harbors, and education, all of which contribute to commerce and the functioning of the market.

Smith wanted greater investment in human capital via education. Without such efforts Smith feared that most people would be poor and would have mindless jobs. Also, he hoped that education would lead to more innovations, possibly generated by workers themselves, and increase productivity.

Smith believed firmly that limited laissez-faire capitalism would be a better, more egalitarian system than mercantilism. Smith's goal was to create a society that was so productive that there would be enough for the "slothful and oppressive profusion of the great, and at the same time abundantly to supply the wants of the artisan, the laborer, and the peasant." In these words we see Smith's disdain for the rich and powerful of his era, and his hope that capitalism would lead to a better world.

Such an idealistic vision was very powerful, especially in the face of ongoing problems of the mercantilist economies. The mercantilist governments in England had attempted to alleviate the plight of the poor with a series of welfare programs and wage subsidies beginning around 1600, but these programs came under attack in the early 1800s with the rise of the philosophy of laissez-faire.

4.4 FROM SUPPORTING THE POOR TO LAISSEZ-FAIRE CAPITALISM

Poor Laws

The expansion of markets under mercantilism was accompanied by major economic problems. Most important was the vast amount of poverty created when the peasants were thrown off their land by the enclosure movement. The poverty often provoked crime, food riots, and other desperate acts by the poor. To reduce some of the negative consequences, England established the Poor Laws beginning around 1600 to ensure that the poor had enough food to survive. These laws were continued in various forms until 1834.

The Speenhamland system, for example, was established in 1795 to reduce rural poverty at a time when high grain prices were making the situation of the poor even more tenuous. Speenhamland subsidized wages based on the price of bread in order to guarantee a minimum income, a "living wage," to the poor irrespective of their earnings. In essence, any worker who received less than a living wage would receive a subsidy from the government up to a minimum level necessary to support a family. The problem with the Speenhamland system was that it eroded incentives. Workers had no reason to work hard. If their pay was slashed because they slacked off on the job, they would then receive a higher subsidy from the government to compensate for their lower wages. Employers had an incentive to pay workers less than a living wage because the government would subsidize low wages until they reached a living wage. The result was that productivity declined and the cost to taxpayers of the Speenhamland system became higher and higher.

In addition to the lower productivity and increasing cost of the Speenhamland system, Thomas Malthus, a minister and influential writer on economics, helped erode support for aiding the poor with his theory of population. Malthus argued that the population would expand as long as there was sufficient food available. Furthermore, he argued that the limited amount of land available could only produce enough food for a certain number of people. With a limited supply of food and an ever-increasing population, Malthus thought famine was inevitable.

Many members of the British Parliament used the population theory of Malthus to argue that giving money to the poor would only lead them to have more children and cause a famine. To eliminate this possibility, Parliament passed the Poor Law Reform Act of 1834, which eliminated relief for the poor except for those who were disabled and created an unregulated market for labor. Subsidies for the poor were replaced by a competitive labor market, and anyone who could not find a job was thrown into a harsh workhouse. No longer was there a commitment to help those who fell upon hard times. Instead, the poor and the unemployed, and often their children, were subject to the brutal treatment of the workhouse. These were the conditions described by Charles Dickens in *Oliver Twist* after visiting a series of workhouses (see Figure 4.3). Even those who worked in factories faced a harsh environment, as we will see in the next chapter.

FIGURE 4.3 "Oliver Asks for More," by George Cruikshank.

It is unfortunate that the hardships of the poor after 1834 in England were a product of bad economic theory. Modern economic research has proven that when the poor have higher incomes and more opportunities they tend to have fewer (not more) children. Families that have lower incomes and are less secure tend to have more children because the extra labor is helpful and the children might earn enough money to support their parents once they reach old age. For poor families in countries without secure retirement benefits, children are the primary provider of security for the elderly. Thus, the removal of support for the poor was based on faulty perceptions of the relationship between incomes for the poor and population growth.

Say's Law and macroeconomic intervention

Laissez-faire policies were also promoted in England in another key area in the early 1800s: Macroeconomic policy. Malthus and a few other economists were worried about the instability of the macroeconomy, which was experiencing frequent recessions; when spending and investment fell, products piled up on store shelves (gluts of goods), and unemployment increased as businesses laid off workers due to slack demand for their products. Despite the problem of frequent recessions, most politicians and economists were convinced by the arguments of Jean-Baptiste Say, who popularized and extended Smith's argument that a capitalist economy was fundamentally stable over the long term.

The key theory in *Say's "law of markets"* was that **supply creates its own demand**. When entrepreneurs make a product, they hire workers, rent land, and buy raw materials, putting money into the hands of workers, landowners, and input suppliers. The money they pay for raw materials becomes income for those businesses, which goes to pay their wages, rent, and materials costs. Businesses also generate profits, which becomes the owners' income. Thus, the act of producing and supplying goods and services generates wages for laborers, rent for landowners, and profits for owners. What do people do with this income? They buy the goods and services that are produced. This is the famous circular flow of economic activity depicted in Figure 4.4.

According to Say's Law, the income from producing goods and services generates exactly enough money to buy those goods and services.

Say's Law is based on a number of crucial assumptions about how the economy works. Recall from Chapter 2 that a model is only as good as its underlying assumptions, and when the assumptions fail the model is usually inaccurate. The **assumptions behind Say's Law** are the following:

1. Consumers' demand for goods and services is unlimited because they get satisfaction from consumption, so they always tend to spend most of their incomes.

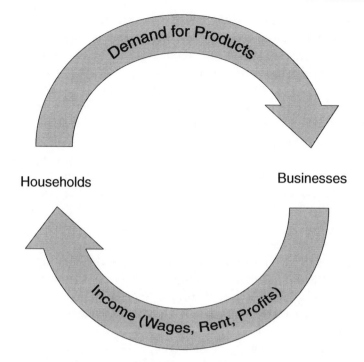

FIGURE 4.4 The simple circular flow model of the economy.

2. An unregulated capitalist system will generate enough income for consumers to buy everything that is produced.
3. All money that is saved or earned as profits will be invested by entrepreneurs due to the (almost unlimited) profitable opportunities provided by capitalism.
4. Wages, prices, and interest rates will adjust very rapidly so that supply
will equal demand.
5. The (standard) *ceteris paribus* assumption holds; All other relevant
factors do not change.

If all of these assumptions hold, then it is likely that enough income is generated to produce enough demand to buy all of the goods that are supplied.
There may be temporary downturns in the economy, but these should be
short-lived. Therefore, economists following Say's Law believed that no
government intervention was necessary in recessions since they thought
that the market would fix itself quickly.

As we will see in more detail later, there are several fundamental
flaws with Say's Law. For now, we will focus on one crucial problem:
The view that there will always be enough demand for products. This
flaw was pointed out by Malthus, Marx, and Keynes but ignored by most
economists until the Great Depression of the 1930s. What economists

now know is that, in recessions, consumers are reluctant to spend because they are worried about keeping their jobs, and businesses are reluctant to invest when they are pessimistic about future sales. Consumer demand and businesses investment purchases both fall, tending to stay low until confidence returns. Pessimistic consumers reduce spending and save more. If the extra money that consumers saved in banks were then spent by businesses on investment goods, the economy would not experience a prolonged recession. However, economic research indicates that *the most important determinant of business investment is expected sales*: Businesses are only willing to buy new machinery and equipment to expand the size of their operations if they think that they will be able to sell more goods in the future. Certainly this is not the case if consumers are buying less goods than normal. Say and most economists of his era assumed that there would always be enough opportunities that businesses would want to invest all the money available in the banking system. In reality, when the business environment is poor and expected sales are low, businesses tend to reduce their investment spending. Money piles up in banks, which are then unable to loan out all the money in their vaults. Even if banks lower their interest rates on loans, businesses are reluctant to borrow money to invest as long as they believe they will not be able to sell all of the products that they produce. One of the key implications is that if businesses expect a bad economy in the future, they reduce investment right away, which then helps to create the bad economy that they expected! Hence, we see that recessions occur regularly due to shortages in demand.

Despite the major flaw in Say's Law, most economists subscribed to this theory and believed that the market would always fix itself very rapidly. They believed that no government intervention was necessary to alleviate unemployment and stimulate a stagnant economy because those problems would always be promptly righted by the market system. Another economic dogma of the economists of this era was the belief in unregulated ("free") trade, based on the theory of comparative advantage developed by David Ricardo.

Free trade and comparative advantage

Under the mercantilist system, trade was heavily protected and imported goods faced stiff tariffs. Given the importance of agriculture to mercantilist economies, agriculture was one of the most protected sectors. In England, the Corn Laws established a high domestic price of grains (corn, wheat) to generate wealth for landlords. However, entrepreneurs and workers objected to the high cost of food, which had the effect of raising wages because workers had to be paid more in order to survive.

David Ricardo argued that England should deregulate trade. That would allow entrepreneurs to earn greater profits, which would be reinvested as purchases of capital goods, which would stimulate economic growth and make everyone better off. According to Ricardo's (1817) Theory of Comparative Advantage, which we will study in more detail later, if all countries engaged in unregulated trade, each country would end up producing the goods that it was relatively best at producing. The competition of the market once tariff protections were eliminated would lead to the most efficient firms surviving, and it would decrease the costs of all goods, which would raise everyone's standard of living. Also, if firms could sell to a larger market, including domestic and foreign consumers, they could increase their level of specialization, which would then increase productivity, as Smith had argued. The result would (in theory) be an economy with more rapid economic growth and a higher standard of living than under regulated (mercantilist) trade.

The Corn Laws were repealed in 1846 based on Ricardo's arguments, marking the completion of England's transition to a grand experiment: Laissez-faire capitalism. Under this economic system, the economic power no longer resided with the merchants and the king. Instead, the most powerful individuals were the entrepreneurial factory owners, and the factory became the center of economic life.

4.5 THE RISE OF THE FACTORY AND THE "DOUBLE MOVEMENT"

Once the Industrial Revolution was underway, it quickly became self-sustaining. The earliest entrepreneurs made huge sums of money, which they invested in new ventures. Many of these new ventures were successful, generating additional profits to be reinvested. As this process continued, the factory came to be the center of the economy, transforming the commercial, agricultural, mercantilist system into a more urban, industrial capitalist system. The pace of change was breathtaking. In 40 years, Glasgow was transformed from a sleepy farming center to an industrial powerhouse with 100 mills producing manufactured goods, iron, leather, chemicals, and more.

By the mid-1800s, many factory owners were wealthy and politically powerful. The factory was the most important institution in the community, determining what life was like for much of the population. Unfortunately for many workers, the transition to factory life was a difficult one. Agrarian peasants did not have an easy life, but they worked at their own pace, and there were times of the year when they did not have to work much, especially in the winter. In the unregulated factories of early capitalism, the pace of work was dictated by the machine, and the work hours pushed people to the brink of human endurance.

So horrific were the conditions that in the late 1700s and early 1800s workers regularly smashed machines and burned factories as part of the Luddite movement. However, the Luddites were arrested and many were hanged in 1813. In essence, the factory system was imposed on a resisting population by force and by the lack of viable alternatives for a poor and desperate population.

If we reflect on the major trends in the development of the market system, we see that national markets were initially created by mercantilist firms and monarchs in pursuit of gold and power. However, the expansion of markets was actively resisted by guilds and workers who sought to maintain their standard of living in any way they could, often using violence. Similarly, as England moved to manufacturing factories and laissez-faire capitalism in the 1800s, workers resisted the horrific conditions, as we will see in the next chapter. Along with the workers' movements, laws regulating factories and various forms of social legislation began to be introduced to mitigate the worst effects of industrial capitalism.

This process of the relentless expansion of markets into new areas at the behest of the most powerful economic interests, coupled with the resistance of workers and communities to market expansion that threatened their livelihood, has been termed "the double movement" by Karl Polanyi. More specifically, the *double movement* describes how **the push for the development of markets by businesses** (first mercantilists and then capitalists) **was met by a counter movement by workers and communities to regulate markets** to prevent them from doing too much destruction to society.

In many ways, early capitalism was, indeed, an ugly thing, and it provoked strong reactions from those it victimized. This is the form of capitalism that Karl Marx described when he wrote, "Capital comes [into the world] dripping from head to foot, from every pore, with blood and dirt." We turn to Marx and workers' resistance to the dark ages of capitalism in the next chapter.

4.6 CONCLUSION

Capitalism began in England based on set of unique institutions that help us to understand the crucial ingredients in a capitalist economic system. The key institutions include a money-driven, scientifically-oriented culture, secure property rights, and a large domestic and colonial market.

The successes of the early capitalists prompted Adam Smith to write *The Wealth of Nations*, in which he proposed that lightly regulated market capitalism would improve the wellbeing of all people. To Smith, the great evils of mercantilism—monopolies and government manipulation of markets for the elites—would be eliminated via the installation of a competitive capitalist system. Competition, moral sentiments, and a sound legal system would, he thought, harness the power of self-interest to generate rapid economic growth that would raise the standard of living for all.

Smith was followed by Say, who argued against the need for government to intervene in recessions, and Ricardo, who argued in favor of unregulated trade with other countries. These powerful ideas, coupled with the elimination of the Poor Laws, resulted in the installation of the world's first laissez-faire capitalist economic system in England between 1834 and 1846. Yet, as England was moving towards laissez-faire capitalism, a counter-movement grew in opposition to capitalism, a phenomenon that Karl Polanyi described as the "double movement."

* *

QUESTIONS FOR REVIEW

1. What were the major institutional factors that spurred the development of capitalism in England? Which of these factors do you think was most important? Why?
2. Given the institutional factors that provided the foundation for capitalism in England, do you think capitalism would work as effectively in other countries with different institutions? Why or why not?
3. Why was Adam Smith critical of mercantilism? Why did he think capitalism was preferable to mercantilism?
4. Smith argued that unregulated (laissez-faire) capitalism would lead to substantial increases in income for all, and especially for workers. Carefully explain how Smith thought this would come about. Critically evaluate his analysis.
5. Smith believed that laissez-faire capitalism would be almost completely self-regulating via the invisible hand, as long as moral sentiments and an effective legal system were in place. Evaluate his argument and use examples of current events to support your analysis.
6. Smith was an opponent of mercantilist governments. What role (if any) does Adam Smith envision for government in a capitalist economy?
7. Why did Malthus (and others) oppose the Poor Laws such as the Speenhamland system? What parts of their arguments were valid and what parts would modern economists consider invalid?

8. Describe Say's Law and why it is important. Also explain the major criticism of Say's Law.

9. Apply Say's Law to the modern economy. Has the economy recently experienced a shortfall in demand, or has the economy operated smoothly without such a problem in recent decades?

10. Why did Smith and Ricardo advocate unregulated trade? What problems might occur when a country moves to unregulated trade? Do we see any such problems in the modern world?

11. Define Karl Polanyi's concept of the double movement and apply this concept to the modern world. Do we see businesses pushing for fewer regulations and access to more markets today? Is there opposition to these business initiatives from people and communities? Give specific examples.

Karl Marx and the dark ages of capitalism

Historical materialism, surplus value, and the exploitation of labor

By the mid-1800s, unregulated capitalism dominated economic systems of Europe and the United States. Adam Smith had hoped that unregulated capitalism would benefit workers, but this was not the case. Instead, this was the dark ages of capitalism: Children were sometimes shackled to machines to keep them at their jobs; workers regularly lost limbs on the job, at which point they were fired since they were no longer productive; work hours were pushed to the brink of human endurance so that laborers spent almost every waking minute working; and work was mind-numbingly dull and repetitive for most industrial laborers.

In this context, Karl Marx wrote his famous critique of capitalism, advocating socialism and communism as alternatives. Although Marx is often thought of as the father of communism, he had very little to say about communism and how it might work. Instead, he concentrated on analyzing the functioning of capitalism.

As we will see, even though he wrote in the mid-1800s, Marx was able to anticipate many of the characteristics of modern capitalism. His analysis predicted, among other things, globalization, the rise of huge corporations, the influence of money in democratic political systems, the abiding alienation of wage workers, and much more. The power of the analytical framework he developed accounts for why many of his ideas still remain relevant today.

This chapter begins by describing the spread of capitalism from England to the U.S. and Europe, and the horrible conditions that characterized capitalism of the mid-1800s. We then turn to Marx's ideas regarding the evolution of economic systems and his analysis of capitalism.

5.0 CHAPTER 5 LEARNING GOALS

After reading this chapter you should be able to:

- Define and give an example of an infant industry promotion strategy;
- Describe the conditions of workers in the 1800s, assess the implications of these conditions for the functioning of laissez-faire capitalism, and determine whether or not you think laissez-faire capitalism inevitably results in exploitation;
- Explain the components of historical materialism, Marx's method of analysis, and apply this method to the evolution of economic systems;
- Use the concept of surplus value to analyze the functioning of a capitalist economic system;
- Evaluate Marx's views on competition and commodification using specific examples from history and from modern capitalism; and,
- Explain the forces in capitalism that Marx thought would result in a workers' revolution and the factors that mitigated those pressures.

5.1 INFANT INDUSTRY PROTECTION AND THE SPREAD OF CAPITALISM IN EUROPE AND THE UNITED STATES

Beginning in the 1300s, England had enacted policies to develop the wool industry. They used measures such as protective tariffs, subsidies and the poaching of skilled workers from foreign manufacturers to give their industry an advantage. This classic approach to economic development is known as an *infant industry promotion strategy*, in which **a country protects and subsidizes a new industry until it can be globally competitive.** In the 1700s, England used similar policies to promote additional industries. By the 1800s, England was the world's technological and industrial leader, and its shift to free trade policies in 1846 was designed to cement the advantages of British industries and undermine the development of competing industries among its European rivals. When you are the global leader with the most efficient industries, free trade benefits your economy while undercutting the industries of other countries.

Most other countries followed England's example, protecting new industries until they could compete with the established industries of other countries. The United States used infant industry promotion strategies once it was independent from England in 1780. Alexander Hamilton, a founding father and the country's first Secretary of the Treasury, successfully persuaded the U.S. Congress to install protective tariffs to allow U.S.

industries to develop and compete with British industries. In Germany, the state provided subsidies and established a number of factories itself. The French hired skilled British workers and engaged in industrial espionage to close the technological gap with Britain. In country after country, governments protected and encouraged industrial development to stimulate the economy and to catch up with the technological leaders. Only small countries such as Switzerland, that were already technologically developed and that needed to sell to larger markets in other countries, pursued free trade policies as they were industrializing.

But as capitalist industries spread to Europe and across the globe, they were accompanied by horrific working conditions. The rosy scenario that Adam Smith anticipated, where the growth of competitive capitalism would dramatically improve the welfare of workers and the poor, did not play out as he had hoped.

5.2 THE CONDITIONS OF WORKERS UNDER CAPITALISM IN THE 1800S

The scores of impoverished people created by England's enclosure movement meant that many people were desperate for work. As a result of the large surplus of laborers, workers had no bargaining power with employers because they could be easily replaced. Consequently, workers had to accept whatever wages and working conditions were offered. And, as noted previously, the earliest entrepreneurs were hard men, uncertain in their ability to make a profit, and driven to squeeze every drop of profit out of their operations. The result was that working and living conditions for the average person were incredibly horrific.

Consider some of the following characteristics of work in England, the wealthiest country in the world in the mid-1800s.

- Employers often preferred women and children for manufacturing work because they were more submissive. Children of the working class began to work as young as 4 years old. They worked for 14–18 hours every day, or until they dropped from exhaustion. Sometimes they were chained to machines and beaten to keep them working. Figure 5.1 depicts Addie Card, a 12-year-old cotton mill worker in 1910.[1]
- There were very few safety precautions, and workers regularly lost fingers, hands, arms, and legs in industrial accidents. Upon experiencing a debilitating injury, workers were usually fired and received no compensation or medical care from their employer.

FIGURE 5.1 Addie Card in 1910.

- Once at the factory, workers had no control over their lives. Breaks were limited to a few minutes each day, despite the incredibly long workdays. Factory owners and managers regularly took sexual advantage of female employees.

As businesses sought to expand markets and gain access to additional resources there was a countermovement to regulate the worst excesses of markets (Polanyi's double movement, for example, as discussed in Chapter 4). But the reforms themselves were modest, and they confirm the overall ugly state of affairs. As a brief example, consider some of the following child labor "reforms" in England:

- 1819, the employment of children under the age of 9 was prohibited in cotton mills;
- 1833, the work week for children under the age of 18 was limited to 69 hours;
- 1842, children under the age of 10 were prohibited from working in coal mines; and,
- 1847, the workday for women and children was limited to 10.5 hours.

The low wages paid by the factories also resulted in squalid living conditions for working class families. Most families lived in single room apartments.

They often could not afford clothes, furniture, or even food. Many people died from disease or malnutrition. To give but a few examples of the human toll of this system, the life expectancy in the manufacturing city of Manchester, England in the mid-1800s was only 17 years. J. C. Symons, a government commissioner, described a working-class neighborhood in Glasgow in 1839 in this way:

> The wynds of Glasgow house a fluctuating population of between 15,000 and 30,000 persons. This district is composed of many narrow streets and square courts and in the middle of each court there is a dung-hill. Although the outward appearance of these places was revolting, I was nevertheless quite unprepared for the filth and misery that were to be found inside. In some of these bedrooms we visited at night we found a whole mass of humanity stretched out on the floor. There were often 15 to 20 men and women huddled together, some being clothed and others naked. Their bed was a heap of musty straw mixed with rags. There was hardly any furniture there and the only thing which gave these holes the appearance of a dwelling was fire burning on the hearth. Thieving and prostitution are the main sources of income of these people... In this part of Glasgow most of the houses have been condemned by the Court of Guild as dilapidated and uninhabitable – but it is just these dwellings which are filled to overflowing, because, by law no rent can be charged on them.[2]

The squalid conditions led to regular outbreaks of cholera, typhoid, and other diseases.

Not surprisingly, the dreadful working and living conditions prompted regular uprisings. Various types of riots and rebellions occurred in England in most years between 1811 and 1850. And yet, employers saw no need to address the desperate conditions of their workers. Their belief was that, once an employer had paid employees their wages, he had no further obligation to them. This was the embodiment of the laissez-faire, every-man-for-himself philosophy that dominated the business community in the early stages of capitalism.

It was in response to this world that Karl Marx wrote his critique of capitalism.

5.3 KARL MARX, HISTORICAL MATERIALISM, AND CLASS CONFLICT

Karl Marx, pictured in Figure 5.2, was born in 1818 into a German economy that was structured to funnel almost all of the resources to the rich.

FIGURE 5.2 Karl Marx (1818–1883).

As in England, German factories were organized in a brutal, militaristic structure designed to discipline and exploit desperate workers. They could do so with impunity due to the support of the government and the elites. Outraged by this society, Marx gravitated towards radical politics during his university years, where he studied philosophy and earned a Ph.D. at age 23. Due to his radical politics, Marx was unable to secure a teaching position, and he was thrown out of Germany, France, and Brussels for his activism on behalf of workers. He eventually settled in England, where he collaborated with Friedrich Engels (1820-1895). Note that Engels acknowledged Marx as the major thinker behind their writings, so most economists attribute the ideas of their co-authored works to Marx.

In 1848, Marx and Engels wrote one of their most powerful documents, *The Communist Manifesto*. In it, they encouraged workers to rise up against their exploitative employers. They also developed a powerful theory of historical change featuring class conflict and technology as the driving factors behind the major shifts in society.

Marx was interested in understanding and analyzing historical change. Adam Smith wrote about capitalism as if it would always operate in a particular way, with small, competitive firms acting to enhance the well-being of society. Marx, however, observed that no economic system was permanent, and within each economic system were forces that threatened to break it apart, sometimes resulting in a new economic system. Marx cited historical evidence indicating that the driving force of the major changes in economic systems was class conflict. Marx and Engels began *The Communist Manifesto* with a famous statement regarding the importance of class conflict to historical change:

> The history of all hitherto existing society is the history of class struggles. Freeman and slave, patrician and plebeian, lord and serf, guildmaster and journeyman, in a word, oppressor and oppressed, stood in constant opposition to one another, carried on an uninterrupted, now hidden, now open fight, a fight that each time ended, either in a revolutionary reconstitution of society at large, or in the common ruin of the contending classes... Our epoch, the epoch of the bourgeoisie [capitalists], ... has simplified class antagonisms. Society as a whole is more and more splitting up into two great hostile camps, into two great classes directly facing each other—Bourgeoisie and Proletariat [workers].

Marx focused on the contradictions within each economic system which would eventually force the system to change. This **method of analysis, focusing on contradictions and the struggle of opposing forces,** is known as ***dialectics***.

Consider for a moment how powerful Marx's observation on class conflict is in helping us to understand the major shifts in economic systems. In each major shift in economic systems—Roman Empire to feudalism, feudalism to mercantilism, and mercantilism to capitalism—class antagonisms featured prominently. For example, the clash of the feudal elites (lords and church officials) with kings and merchants destroyed feudalism and ushered in mercantilism, as kings and merchants reshaped society based on their interests in extending markets. With their rise in power and importance, capitalists were able to prevail against the interests of merchants and kings and replace mercantilism with laissez-faire capitalism. And, as we shall see later, the conflict between capitalists and workers under laissez-faire capitalism produced the mixed-market capitalist economies of the modern world. In each case, an economic system was unable to resolve major conflicts over resources in society, resulting in conflicts between key classes and leading to a new type of economic system.

Technology also plays an important role in reshaping economic systems. The development of agriculture prompted the change from hunter-gatherer societies to agriculture-based empires. The rise in agricultural productivity during feudalism promoted urbanization and trade and established conditions that were ripe for mercantilism. The development of shipping, guns, and steel in Europe made mercantilism and colonial empires possible. The steam engine stimulated the development of factories in early capitalism. In all of these examples, technological changes prompted changes in class structures, which helped to undermine existing class relations.

Given that no economic system has lasted forever and that there are many conflicts and technological changes occurring in contemporary society, think for a moment about how the next economic system might arise and what it might look like:

- What do you see as the major contradictions in our current society?
- What technological changes are fundamentally reshaping society?
- What are the key social classes engaged in conflicts over resources?
- What type of economic system might emerge from these contradictions, changes, and conflicts?

Identifying the major contradictions, technological changes, and conflicts helps us to identify the major sources of change in an economic system. Conflicts, which arise from contradictions and technological changes that advantage some groups over others, often drive major changes. Marx focused on the fight over economic resources as the primary source of conflict because, historically, this battle has been the most important factor behind changes in economic systems. Also, the **material conditions** of society are the primary influence on what our lives are like, determining who we interact with during most of the day, how hard we have to work, our status in society, who we are likely to marry, and so on.

For example, what social class you are born into has a huge influence on what your life will be like, affecting whether or not you are likely to go to an elite college, if you are more likely to end up working on Wall Street or at Wal-Mart, and if you are likely to be a manager or a laborer. The **relations of production** are the relationships between people in the workplace, and they are primarily determined by your social class.

Also important in shaping the conditions of society are technological factors, including tools, machinery, infrastructure, resources, labor power, and knowledge. These Marx called the **forces of production**. The physical, non-human parts of the forces of production, including machinery, tools, buildings, infrastructure, and natural resources, are called the **means of production**. In a capitalist economic system, capitalists own and control the means of production while workers have to sell their labor to capitalists in order to survive. Together, the forces of production (technology, knowledge) and the (class) relations of production are the driving forces behind the changes in society. **Marx's approach to the study of economics, focusing on the class conflicts and technological changes that provoke changes in the material conditions of society over time, is called *historical materialism.***

Marx turned his sophisticated analytical method to the study of the laissez-faire capitalist system of the mid-1800s. Where Smith saw profit-seeking as a positive force, Marx saw a system that brutalized workers and turned everything—people, love, religion, democracy, justice—into a commodity to be bought and sold. The key to understanding how exploitation and commodification come about is Marx's concept of surplus value.

5.4 SURPLUS VALUE AND THE EXPLOITATION OF LABOR

In the capitalist system of the mid-1800s there were two main social classes, the capitalists who owned the means of production and the workers who were forced to sell their labor. During Marx's era, the small middle class that existed, consisting of skilled craftspeople and owners of small shops, was being rapidly displaced by the ever-growing capitalist firms. Thus, Marx concentrated on the two main social classes of his day, capitalists and workers.

The main dynamic between capitalists and workers is shaped by the pursuit of profit by the capitalist. In a competitive capitalist system, owners are forced to be "hard men" who extract the most they can from their business. In the cutthroat capitalist world, if you can't produce the best product for the lowest possible price, then you will likely get displaced by a competitor who is better or more efficient. And, you must constantly reinvest your profits in new ventures and new technology to stay one step ahead of your competitors. Indeed, the reinvestment of profits into new production techniques and products is usually the key to long-term survival. Thus, in order to survive, firms must keep costs as low as possible and accumulate sufficient profits for reinvestment. These profits are invested in capital goods (machinery, equipment, research and development, etc.), resulting in capital accumulation (a larger and larger capital stock). Marx saw capital accumulation as one of the key forces in capitalism, driving the development of new products, the search for new markets, and the exploitation of labor.

In their relentless pursuit of profit (and capital accumulation), firms have to extract as much effort as possible at as low a wage as possible from their workers. In other words, firms seek the maximum production from workers for the lowest cost.

To demonstrate this fundamental aspect of capitalism, Marx developed a simple model of the workday based on the concept of **surplus value**. During the first part of the workday, the worker produces goods or services to generate enough profits to pay for their wages (and benefits) for the day. Once a worker has paid for his or her wages, the rest of the work for the day generates profits for the owner. Thus the workday can be broken down into the following:

$$A\,-----------------\,B\,------------\,C,$$

where A—B pays for the wage and B—C is profit (surplus value).

Surplus value is defined as **the amount of value produced by workers over and above the cost of their wages (including benefits).**

In this relationship, a firm that is pursuing maximum profits must increase the B—C part of the workday as much as possible. That can be done in two different ways:

1. Increasing the length of the workday (moving C to the right from C to C_2, as shown in Figure 5.3); and,
2. Reducing the amount of time necessary to pay for a laborer's wage (moving B to the left from B to B_2, as shown in Figure 5.3). This can be done by (a) reducing wages, (b) replacing workers with more cost-effective machinery, or (c) increasing the productivity of workers by speeding up the pace of work or other measures that target productivity.

This is where the fight over the workday in capitalism arises. Clearly, employers want to maximize profits, and that means getting the most surplus value possible from their workers. Once employers have paid their workers' daily salaries, the incentive is to work them as many hours as possible. And employers always want to pay the lowest wages possible.

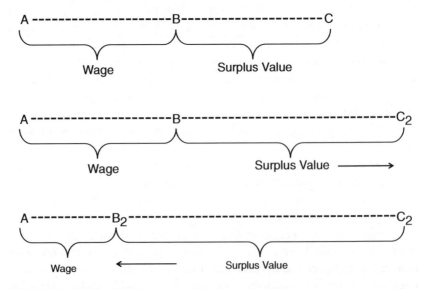

FIGURE 5.3 The fight over the workday.

But what do workers want? Mostly, they prefer just the opposite: Workers want higher pay and shorter hours.

During the years of unregulated capitalism, factory owners went to great lengths to increase their profits and undercut their competitors. With daily wages fixed, employers engaged in relentless efforts to expand work hours, as documented in Juliet Schor's (1991) book, *The Overworked American*:

- The invention of artificial lighting was used to increase work from daylight hours (about 12 hours a day) to as many as 16 hours a day.
- Meal times and breaks were shortened to only a few minutes each day.
- Holidays and days off were eliminated.
- Clocks at factories were set ahead in the morning and turned back at night to manipulate laborers into working more hours. Workers, who usually did not own watches and who lived in fear of beatings or being fired, could only accept these manipulations.

In the mid-1800s, factory work hours reached between 75 and 90 a week in England and the U.S. As a show of how much power employers had, they challenged human endurance by pushing work hours to extremes.

In addition to extending work hours, employers sought to increase surplus value in other ways. They tried to reduce wages by employing children and women instead of men, using slave labor if it was allowed, and moving operations to locations where wages were lower. They replaced workers with machinery that was less costly. In particular, they replaced highly paid skilled laborers with less skilled workers using machines, which resulted in considerable cost savings. Additionally, they increased the pace of work by speeding up assembly lines and closely supervising workers. For example, Frederick Taylor (1856–1915) developed factory systems in which every motion of every worker was monitored and controlled for optimum efficiency.

Marx saw the relationship between capitalists and workers as fundamentally exploitative. First, employers have more power than workers in the market for labor. Employers control the amount of jobs, and they are able to select from an abundant supply of workers. As long as there are surplus workers around, workers have to accept the conditions set by the employer. Marx called the chronic surplus of workers the **reserve army of the unemployed,** and he noted that having a ready supply of disciplined, desperate, unemployed laborers was very useful to capitalists. Unemployment helps to push wages down and to keep workers in line due to their fears of being replaced by an unemployed person. Also, the unemployed provide a ready pool of labor if a firm needs to expand the size of its operations.

Second, surplus value is exploitative because if a worker owned the business herself, she would get to keep the surplus value instead of having it seized by the capitalist. Surplus value goes to whoever owns the business (the means of production). But why do capitalists own the factory instead of workers? In the 1800s, most wealth could be traced back to the era when resources (especially land) were seized in the enclosure movement, establishing a wealthy class that in turn became factory owners. To Marx, ownership of factories and businesses was usually a product of the theft of public resources or luck of birth, so he saw the seizure of surplus value as an exploitative and unjustified act. It was this idea—that private property was born out of theft and exploitation—that led Marx to advocate a socialist or communist system in which workers would own and control the factories.

Workers, of course, resisted the extension of work hours, intensification of work, and efforts to reduce wages in any way they could. When workers functioned as individuals, they were expendable and had little power. But when they joined together to form labor unions, they were able to demand changes. Their major weapon was the strike: When all workers refused to work at the same time, they could bring production to a halt. When workers were united and when employment conditions were favorable (a high demand for labor to produce goods during an economic boom), workers were able to demand shorter hours, better conditions, and higher pay. This is exactly what Marx and Engels were arguing when they ended *The Communist Manifesto* with their famous call-to-arms: "Workers of the world, unite! You have nothing to lose but your chains!"

Marx was describing capitalism of the mid-1800s, but it is worth noting the extent to which the processes he described are still visible in modern capitalism. Every year, firms such as Wal-Mart are convicted of forcing laborers to work off the clock (work for no pay). Employers increasingly demand that workers be available evenings and weekends for work. Firms still shift their operations around the globe in search of cheaper, more vulnerable workers. They continue to replace skilled labor with mechanization and less skilled workers. They also monitor workers to keep them on task and working efficiently.

Nothing indicates the enduring importance of the idea of surplus value more strongly than the modern employment relationship. Ask yourself, "When I graduate from college, why will a company want to hire me?" The answer, as Marx noted so many years ago, is, "Because you will make the company more money than you will cost them." In other words, you will produce profit (surplus value), which your employer gets to keep. If you ever find yourself in a situation where you cost your employer more money than you make them, you can expect to be cast into the reserve army of the unemployed.

The power of Marx's concept of surplus value can also be seen in the major trends that Marx predicted in modern capitalism. These include Marx's view of competition as a race to the bottom, and his predictions of globalization, the concentration of capital and the commodification of most aspects of life.

5.5 MARX ON COMPETITION, GLOBALIZATION, ECONOMIC CONCENTRATION, AND COMMODIFICATION

As noted above, Adam Smith saw competition as a positive force in the economy, keeping firms innovative, prices low, and demand for workers high. Marx, however, saw a darker side to capitalist competition. Marx acknowledged that the Industrial Revolution and the capitalist economic system that sparked it had generated impressive amounts of new products and worthwhile inventions. But the effect on workers had not been the rosy scenario Smith had laid out, with upstanding, moral employers creating better and better conditions for workers. Instead, many workers were worse off under capitalism than they had been under feudalism.

The problem was that competition also put pressures on firms to engage in the most ruthless, merciless practices possible. If one employer found it cheaper to use child laborers rather than adults, other firms would follow suit or be out-competed and out of business. If one employer spent less money on worker safety and extracted more work out of each worker, that employer could undercut the competition. In essence, competition served as a race to the bottom, with each firm forced to sink to the level of the least scrupulous firm in the market.

In a competitive, laissez-faire, market economy, employers could not adhere to their moral beliefs as Smith hoped. Instead, they were forced to adopt the morals of their least ethical, most merciless competitor in order to survive. In other words, Marx saw competition as a **race to the bottom**.

This is another of Marx's insights that still has relevance. To give a modern example, for most of its history, Levi Strauss prided itself on being a socially responsible company that manufactured jeans in the United States and paid its workers well. But in 1999, it began closing its U.S. factories and using sweatshop labor overseas to manufacture their products. As Levi's CEO Robert Haas stated, despite investing tens of millions of dollars to keep U.S. plants competitive, "We can't swim against the tide." In a throwback to the dark ages of capitalism, Levi's factories abroad were accused of exploiting Chinese prison labor, firing workers who tried to unionize, and forcing laborers to work more than 12 hours per day while withholding overtime pay. Levi's factories in Saipan paid workers $3 an hour, much less than the $18 an hour that U.S. workers earned. While Levi's was one of the last holdouts against using sweatshop labor abroad, they eventually succumbed to the race to the bottom provoked by competitive pressures. They joined the company of firms like Nike, who boasted in the late 1990s that workers in their factories were required to be at least 16 years old and to work no more than 60 hours a week. Evidently Nike considered these employment rules to be a form of progress!

We see many other examples of the race to the bottom in contemporary capitalism. Firms sometimes move operations overseas to escape taxes, labor laws, or environmental regulations. There have been numerous attempts by companies around the globe to bribe government officials so that they do not enforce laws and regulations. The fact that we have had to outlaw child labor, deceptive advertising, unsafe working conditions, hazardous waste dumping, and other unsavory business activities indicates the powerful drive toward the bottom produced by competitive capitalism.

The drive to increase profits is at the root of **globalization**. As Marx and Engels observed in *The Communist Manifesto*, "The need of a constantly expanding market for its products chases the bourgeoisie over the whole surface of the globe. It must nestle everywhere, settle everywhere, establish connections everywhere." The efforts of large multinational firms to establish operations to open markets in China and to gain access to raw materials and labor in Africa, South Asia, and South America demonstrate the ongoing relevance of this part of Marx's analysis.

Another characteristic of capitalist markets that Marx anticipated was the **increasing concentration of capital** into fewer and fewer hands. In other words, Marx predicted the domination of markets by huge companies that would, if allowed, monopolize markets. While Smith hoped that there would always be a sufficient amount of competition, Marx noted that in competition there were winners and losers, and the winning firms would get larger and larger as they swallowed up competitors and used their size as an advantage. One glance at the landscape of modern capitalism reveals the accuracy of Marx's prediction. In each major industry, we see a handful of huge companies dominating: Internet searches and ads (Google), smart phones (Apple, Samsung), breakfast cereals (General Mills, Kellogg, Post), soft drinks (Coke, Pepsi), fast food (McDonald's, Subway, Burger King, Wendy's), pizza (Pizza Hut, Domino's), beer (Budweiser/InBev, SABMiller–Molson Coors), and so on. Some industries are moderately competitive, such as cars (Toyota, General Motors, VW, Hyundai, Ford, Nissan, Fiat Chrysler, Honda) and small retail businesses, but most manufacturing industries are dominated by a few huge firms. If not for anti-trust laws that limit the ability of huge firms to get even larger, it appears that most markets would end up being monopolized because of the advantages that huge firms have. Not only can large firms achieve greater efficiency (greater size leads to greater degrees of specialization and lower costs), but they can use their financial resources to buy up competitors or to snap up the latest innovations, staying atop the heap for long stretches of time.

Marx also observed how economic systems tended to shape the values of society. In capitalism, the emphasis on making money affects everything; or, as Marx put it in 1846, "Money abases all the gods of mankind and changes them into commodities." This is the process of **commodification.** Christianity had been transformed from a religion in which greed was considered to be a sin during feudalism to a religion which celebrated greed and wealth during mercantilism and even more so during capitalism.

Even more destructive was the commodification of labor under capitalism. Instead of seeing workers as human beings, capitalists were forced by competitive pressures to view workers as tools to be used up and then cast aside. The brutal conditions of laissez-faire capitalism, some of which were described above, were evidence of the dehumanizing effect capitalism had on the relationship between workers and owners.

Marx developed the term **alienation** to describe how work under capitalism tended to be unnatural and isolating. In previous human societies, people were usually connected to their work as a farmer or skilled craftsperson. They were connected to nature and to work that was usually social, involved a variety of tasks, and could even be interesting and creative at times. Under capitalism, however, work became isolated, repetitive drudgery. **Deskilling** took place, where skilled craftspeople were replaced by unskilled workers using a machine. These unskilled workers toiled by themselves at a machine for 16 hours a day in a dreary, unsafe factory. It is difficult to imagine a more mind-numbing experience.

Even in modern, regulated capitalism, most workers find their jobs to be alienating. A 2014 Gallup survey asked more than 5 million workers if they found their jobs to be "engaging," by which it meant "involved in, enthusiastic about and committed to their work and workplace." Only 31.5 percent of employees in the survey reported being engaged at work, while 51 percent were not engaged and 17.5 percent were actively discouraged. Drudgery, it seems, is a defining characteristic of work in a capitalist system for most people.

In addition to the commodification of labor, another particularly glaring example is the commodification of holidays and major societal events. If you are the CEO of a company that must generate the maximum amount of profits possible to survive, you have to push for new sales in every way possible. One of the best ways to do this is to connect your product to deep human emotions, such as those associated with love or a religious holiday.

The diamond engagement ring exemplifies the commodification of love under modern capitalism. Human beings have used rings as a symbol of unity for thousands of years. But the widespread use of the diamond engagement ring was a product of a particularly effective marketing campaign by the De Beers Corporation, a South African mining company that controls most of the world's supply of diamonds. In the 1930s, only 10 percent of engagement rings contained diamonds. De Beers began featuring glamourous movie stars adorned in diamonds in movies and magazines. The company emphasized the purity, sparkle, and durability of the diamond as a symbol of a man's love for a woman, and it suggested that men spend 1 month's salary on an engagement ring, putting a very specific price on love! De Beers later raised their definition of the appropriate amount of salary to spend to 2 months in the 1980s. The idea that love and engagement to be married have come to be associated with a specific value and a specific commodity is a classic example of commodification.

Another classic example is the commodification of Christmas. Visitors to the United States from different cultures are often astounded by the various manifestations of Christmas under capitalism. Rather than a religious holiday, it appears to an external observer as an orgy of consumerism in which people are told via a massive advertising effort that if they love someone they should express that love by buying them expensive commodities. The modern messages are very explicit about what you should do for your loved ones at Christmas:

- DeBeers says, "This Christmas go straight for the heart: A diamond is forever."
- A flower company encourages people to "show your loved ones how much you care with a gift from 1800 Flowers."
- Godiva chocolates tells us, "This holiday season give the finest to those you love."
- Hallmark invites us to buy their cards when we "care enough to send the very best."

And, there are a thousand more examples, all equating love, caring and Christmas sentiment with purchasing commodities.

It is also worth noting the extent to which capitalism commodifies public services such as the administration of justice. In the U.S., those who can afford better lawyers are much more likely to get better legal outcomes than those who cannot. Even democracy has been commodified to a significant degree in the U.S., where it takes millions of dollars to mount a political campaign for Congress and a trillion dollars to compete in a Presidential election. More than half of the members of Congress are millionaires. In another perceptive prediction, Marx argued that politicians in a capitalist system would become beholden to the capitalists, and that this would limit the ability of democracy to work on behalf of workers.

The commodification and exploitation of labor led Marx to believe that capitalism was irredeemable. Ultimately, given the corrupt nature of political systems and the brutal conditions of workers, Marx predicted that a workers' revolution was inevitable. He thought that a revolution would likely occur during one of the prolonged economic crises that plagued laissez-faire capitalism.

5.6 CRISIS AND REVOLUTION

Not only was capitalism of the mid-1800s incredibly unequal and exploitative, it was also prone to regular economic crises. To Marx, this was a product of the inherent contradictions in capitalism. On the one hand, capitalists are driven to invest in new machinery and new markets, relentlessly increasing the amount of goods they produce. At the same time, they work as hard as possible to suppress wages and minimize costs. But if output is constantly growing while wages are stagnant or falling, the economy will eventually reach a point where a large supply of goods exists, but workers have limited incomes to buy those goods. The result of too much supply and too little demand is a crisis of underconsumption. As goods sit unsold on store shelves, businesses are forced to cut back on production, resulting in layoffs of workers and increasing poverty, which further undermines spending and ultimately results in a crisis (recession).

Along with experiencing regular crises, capitalism was becoming more unequal during Marx's day; firms were growing larger and a rising number of independent craftspeople were being displaced by capitalist firms. The combination of regular crises and increasing inequality led Marx to believe that some sort of major change was inevitable. He hoped that a revolt of the working class would replace capitalism with socialism, a system in which the means of production would be used for the benefit of all instead of to generate profits for the elite. Moreover, he hoped that once people became more communally minded and less selfish, they might be willing to replace socialism with an even more egalitarian system, communism, in which all of society's resources are shared equally. In a communist system, people would work "each according to their ability" and they would be provided for "each according to their needs."

This is, without question, an idealistic vision. Like Smith, Marx truly wished for an economic system that would create a better life for all, and especially for those who were most exploited under capitalism.

As workers increasingly joined unions and became more powerful, there was talk of revolution, especially in the most unequal societies. However, as we will see in the next chapter, pressure from labor unions and reformers and the severity of the worst crisis in capitalist history, the Great Depression, undermined the credibility of laissez-faire capitalism and ushered in the era of regulated capitalism. As Marx predicted, the combination of a major economic crisis (the Great Depression) and great inequality did result in a change in economic systems. But the new system in Europe and the U.S. was a more humanized form of capitalism rather than socialism. Under pressure, democratic leaders passed laws limiting work hours, promoting worker safety, regulating child labor, and providing a safety net for the poor, the elderly, and the unemployed. Also, encouraged by the ideas of John Maynard Keynes, capitalist countries began successfully engaging in stabilization policies to reduce the length and severity of crises. Additional government spending in recessions helped to put money in peoples' pockets and to put people back to work.

Whereas laissez-faire capitalism was quite unstable, regulated capitalism proved to be more stable, and the gains of regulated capitalism were distributed more widely. The improvement in the conditions of the working class eased the pressures for revolution in the U.S. and Europe. However, the most unequal societies that were not able to spread the wealth more widely, such as Russia, Cuba, and China, proved to be ripe for communist revolutions.

It is important to note that Marx said very little about communism and how it might work. Given that he was throughout his life a tireless advocate of workers' power and wellbeing, it is unlikely that he would have approved of dictatorial communism such as the kind that developed in the Soviet Union. In Soviet Russia, workers were exploited and had very little power and control over their work and lives, much as was the case under unregulated capitalism. In the ultimate irony, the fall of the Soviet Union and the Eastern bloc was sparked by a workers' revolt in Poland led by the Solidarity movement, an independent, self-governing trade union! Thus, it is more correct to consider Marx an astute analyst of laissez-faire capitalism than the architect of totalitarian communism.

5.7 CONCLUSION

Capitalism spread across Europe and the United States in the mid-1800s as countries used infant industry promotion strategies to develop their economies. However, the conditions for workers under laissez-faire capitalism were abhorrent, sparking strikes and other forms of resistance.

It was in this world that Karl Marx developed his sophisticated analysis of capitalism, exposing the contradictory forces within the system that led to rapid growth and development, on the one hand, and utter desperation and poverty for most workers on the other. His method of analysis, historical materialism, and his key analytical concept, surplus value, help us to understand how unregulated capitalism tends to work. In particular, Marx emphasized how competitive pressures all too often produced a race to the bottom, and how the commodification of labor and other key aspects of society would demean and distort labor, culture, justice, and democracy.

Despite the accuracy of many of his predictions, Marx and his ideas were ignored by mainstream economists, who continued to see the market as efficient and effective. However, changes in the structure of capitalism made such views increasingly difficult to maintain. With the rise of the robber barons and huge corporations in the U.S., the era of competitive capitalism was replaced by a new era of monopoly capitalism in the late 1800s and early 1900s. It was in that period that Thorstein Veblen wrote his famous critique of the leisure class and the monopolistic forces that had come to dominate laissez-faire capitalism. In the process, Veblen developed a very sophisticated and useful economic methodology known as institutionalism. Veblen was followed by John Maynard Keynes, probably the most important economist of the 1900s. Keynes founded the study of macroeconomics, which focuses on the large, aggregate forces that shape an economic system. Keynes argued that the worst excesses of capitalism, including the problem of recurring economic crises, could be eliminated with appropriate government intervention. Keynes was opposed by Friedrich Hayek, who feared that any increase in government power would lead to totalitarianism. We turn next to the rise of monopoly capitalism, the ideas of Thorstein Veblen and the Great Depression.

* *

QUESTIONS FOR REVIEW

1. Explain in your own words the concept of an infant industry promotion strategy. Do you think such strategies could work in the modern world? Why or why not?

2. Given the experiences of workers under laissez-faire capitalism, analyze Smith's argument that laissez-faire capitalism would benefit workers. Which of Smith's ideas hold up and which do not?

3. What are the key components of Marx's method, historical materialism? Explain briefly. Use historical materialism to explain the transition from one specific economic system to another.

4. Describe what you see as the major contradictions, technological changes, and class conflicts in our current society. What factors do you think are most likely to provoke a crisis? What type of economic system might evolve out of the crisis to resolve the existing contradictions?

5. List all of the factors that would increase the surplus value going to an employer.

6. Find three examples from a reputable news source that illustrate the drive by modern employers for greater surplus value.

7. Would it be possible for an employer to pay and treat workers well and still increase the amount of surplus value it takes in? Why or why not?

8. Do you or most people you know find work to be alienating? Explain and give specific examples.

9. Find three examples of commodification that you see around you. Choose different examples than those given in this chapter.

10. Contrast Marx's view of competition with Adam Smith's. Analyze which aspects of their views of competition you think are most accurate, and support your answer with specific examples.

11. Explain why Marx thought capitalism would eventually lead to a workers' revolt. Assess the strengths and weaknesses of Marx's argument regarding the inevitable fall of laissez-faire capitalism.

NOTES

1. Source: https://commons.wikimedia.org/wiki/File%3AAddieCard05282vLewis Hine.jpg.

2. Quoted in Friedrich Engels, *The Condition of the Working Class in England*, 1845.

Thorstein Veblen and monopoly capitalism

The rise of manufacturing and the fall of laissez-faire

By the end of the 1800s, capitalist firms had evolved from small, local factories to huge, national corporations. The development of the limited liability corporation in the United States facilitated that change and led to the era of the robber barons. This era is sometimes termed "monopoly capitalism" because industries came to be dominated by huge firms with significant monopoly power. But monopoly capitalism contained within it numerous contradictions. In particular, it was prone to frequent booms and busts and marked by inequality, with fabulous wealth generated for the few, poverty and desperation for the many, and only a small middle class.

Economic divisions were particularly dramatic with respect to race, ethnicity, class, and gender. Despite the abolition of slavery at the end of the U.S. Civil War, African Americans faced racial discrimination on a massive scale. Women continued to be barred from most professions. And workers in the new manufacturing firms faced harsh conditions and an unsympathetic government. Meanwhile, workers in less developed countries endured even worse experiences under imperial rule by European countries, the U.S., and Japan.

During the unrest and unevenness of the economic system of the time, a new approach to studying the economy, neoclassical economics, developed. This approach attempted to be scientific, emulating the approaches of Physics and other sciences, in developing simplified mathematical models of economic behavior. Meanwhile, Thorstein Veblen developed a completely different approach.

Veblen focused on the forces in the economy that cause it to evolve and change, as well as the institutions—the culture, legal system, corporations, government, and other patterns of human interaction—that shape human actions in the economy. Veblen incorporated psychology, anthropology, and history to arrive at a detailed and complex analysis of the economy. As the economy experienced fitful booms and busts and as the elites of the era grew richer and richer, Veblen criticized a system he saw as wasteful, destructive, and fundamentally unfair.

This pinnacle of monopoly capitalism came in the boom of the roaring 1920s, but this was followed by the worst crisis capitalism had ever experienced, the Great Depression. The Depression was so devastating that it caused a fundamental shift in economic systems and in the field of economics.

This chapter starts by describing the evolution of laissez-faire capitalism from small firms to large limited liability corporations in the U.S., and the ideas of Thorstein Veblen regarding this society. Subsequently, we examine race, ethnicity, gender, and imperialism in the U.S. and less developed countries. We then turn to a brief sketch of the ideas of neoclassical economists (who we will study in more depth later), before taking up the ideas of Thorstein Veblen. The chapter concludes with a section on the Great Depression.

6.0 CHAPTER 6 LEARNING GOALS

After reading this chapter you should be able to:

- Describe the rise of U.S. monopoly capitalism and how this system was structured relative to owners, workers, the government, as well as race, gender, ethnicity, and imperialism;
- Explain the approach taken by neoclassical economists and what they were trying to achieve with their approach;
- Define and apply the major concepts developed by Thorstein Veblen: evolution, institutions, culture, pecuniary emulation, conspicuous consumption, making money vs. making goods, and the vested interests; and,
- Describe how the roaring 1920s in the U.S. created the conditions for the Great Depression, and how the Great Depression created the conditions for a new approach to economics.

6.1 THE DEVELOPMENT OF MONOPOLY CAPITALISM IN THE UNITED STATES

When Adam Smith first wrote about capitalism, firms were small and markets primarily local. High transportation costs and the limited size of local markets created conditions favorable for small firms manufacturing and selling goods locally. A series of factors changed the structure of capitalism in the late 1800s. (1) Changes in transportation technology (canals and trains, followed by automobiles) and communication (the telegraph, then the telephone) made it possible to travel and communicate across large distances, creating a national, interconnected market. (2) New manufacturing technologies (steel, chemicals, engines, electricity) allowed large firms who made substantial investments to dominate smaller firms. (3) Laws establishing limited liability corporations promoted investment by insuring that stockholders would receive a share of profits, but the most they could lose would be the amount of their investment and they would not be liable for any debts incurred by the company. (4) The development of the banking sector provided financing for large firms to expand, and larger firms were able to borrow at lower interest rates than smaller firms. (5) Large firms had more influence over the government, and were able to obtain government contracts, subsidies, and protection from foreign competition more easily than small firms. (6) Once a large firm came to dominate an industry, it could raise prices and increase profits, which gave the owners even more money with which to make investments and buy out competition. The **ability to control prices** is defined as ***monopoly power***, and the amount of monopoly power a firm has is directly proportional to its market share.

Industry after industry came to be dominated by a few huge firms. In the early 1800s, no company controlled more than 10 percent of the output in a manufacturing industry. By the early 1900s most industries were dominated by a few large firms, and in more than 160 industries, a single firm produced more than half of the output. United States Steel controlled 85 percent of steel production and Standard Oil owned 95 percent of the oil industry. Companies used size, collusion (forming secret trusts), mergers (buying out competitors), bribes (to get favorable treatment from the government or shipping companies), and even illegal means to dominate their industry.

The story of how Standard Oil came to dominate the oil industry is emblematic of the robber baron era. John D. Rockefeller purchased an oil refinery in Cleveland in 1862. He then merged with and purchased other competitors, forming Standard Oil as a limited liability corporation in 1870. Now that Standard Oil had a degree of monopoly power, Rockefeller began to collude and combine secretly with other large refineries to raise prices and profits, forming the Standard Oil Trust in 1882. Standard Oil used its large size to demand lower shipping costs from the railroads, and the lower costs allowed it to double the size of the company by undercutting competitors. Once it was the dominant company, Rockefeller then demanded that railroads pay Standard Oil rebates whenever they shipped the oil of competitors, and that the railroads share all data from shipments of their competitors, including the buyer and price of the shipment. This gave Rockefeller immense advantages. Rockefeller was also known for bribing and threatening competitors, and Standard Oil officials even arranged for an explosion to occur at a rival refinery.

Other robber barons engaged in similar manipulations. Andrew Carnegie copied the Bessemer method of producing steel from England, built his own huge plant in the U.S., and persuaded Congress to protect the steel industry from foreign competition, making him hundreds of millions of dollars. J. P. Morgan bought up half of the country's railroads along with a series of banks and insurance companies. He eventually bought out Carnegie and formed U.S. Steel. As Howard Zinn described it in A People's History of the United States, "And so it went, in industry after industry—shrewd, efficient businessmen building empires, choking out competition, maintaining high prices, keeping wages low, using government subsidies."[1]

The robber barons made a special point of crushing any attempt by workers to form unions and to get higher pay and better conditions. As in England, work hours were long and working conditions harsh. Workers responded the only way they could, by forming labor unions and going on strike. However, the police, at the urging of employers, responded brutally; striking men, women, and children were shot with disturbing frequency.

The ruthless behavior of the robber barons did provoke resistance from farmers and workers, who increasingly demanded laws to rein in the power of corporations. Also, government officials became worried about the increasing power of corporations as the size of the largest firms became larger than entire states. The Sherman Antitrust Act, passed in 1889, outlawed trusts and conspiracies that would lead to monopolies or otherwise restrain trade. However, the law was twisted by pro-corporation courts from an anti-trust law to a measure to prevent labor unions from striking, and numerous labor leaders were arrested based on the new law. In a similar fashion, many federal regulatory agencies, such as the Interstate Commerce Commission, that were originally charged with regulating industries eventually were manipulated into helping industries make excess profits at the expense of the public. At this point in U.S. history, the duly elected government was operating almost entirely on the side of business, just as Marx predicted it would.

Despite these problems, the U.S. economy became the largest and most advanced in the world under monopoly capitalism. Meanwhile, the working class was not able to effectively counter the power of the robber barons. Divisions that existed with respect to race, ethnicity, and gender made it difficult for the working class in the United States to unite.

6.2 RACE, ETHNICITY, CLASS, AND GENDER IN THE UNITED STATES

Slaves were introduced into the American colonies in 1619, establishing racist exploitation as one of the foundations of the early economic system. Slavery was immensely profitable for plantation owners until the end of the Civil War. James Madison, instrumental in writing the U.S. Constitution, once boasted to "a British visitor shortly after the American Revolution that he could make $257 on every Negro in a year, and spend only $12 or $13 on his keep."[2] However, wealthy landowners feared a revolt by black slaves allied with poor white indentured servants. They began giving whites who completed their period of indentured servitude land, money, and greater status in order to separate their interests from those of black slaves.

In the U.S., wealthy white landowners sat atop the class structure. Underneath them were a small number of free, white merchants and small farmers. Next were white sharecroppers and indentured servants. At the bottom were black slaves. Native Americans were primarily excluded from white society and were thus outside the class system.

Even after the end of slavery after the Civil War, the black population of the United States remained at the bottom rung of society. Although African Americans were no longer slaves, they had no land and no money, so they had little choice other than to work for landowners as sharecroppers: They farmed the owner's land and gave the owner half of what was produced, similar to the system that existed during feudalism in Europe. But the value of the crops they produced was not enough to live on most years, so sharecroppers fell increasingly into debt. In addition to their desperate economic situation, African Americans faced the terroristic violence of the Ku Klux Klan, which tortured, raped and murdered blacks in the southern United States. Furthermore, legal racial segregation established by the "Jim Crow laws" made it difficult for blacks to vote and established segregated schools, transportation, bathrooms, restaurants, drinking fountains, and so on. With such a deep history of racial discrimination, most labor unions actively discriminated against black workers, refusing to let them join white unions.

Ethnic differences also splintered the white working class. In U.S. cities, white immigrants from Ireland, Italy, and other countries faced discrimination and stereotyping, making it difficult for workers to unite. Gender divisions were even more intractable.

Many women worked in factories, but they were paid lower salaries than men. Almost all labor unions excluded women. Women were barred from many professions, especially the highest paid jobs in law and medicine. Additionally, women were still not allowed to vote. As a consequence, an increasingly powerful women's movement lobbied for greater rights and especially the right to vote, which was finally achieved in 1920.

If we fast forward to today, although there is greater class mobility now, the descendants of slaves and indentured servants are more likely to be members of the lower classes than the descendants of the wealthy landowners. Many Native Americans are still separated from white society. Women today are, on average, paid significantly less than men and are less likely to be selected for top positions in corporations and government. The social classes and race and gender structures at the beginning of our history evidently have had a significant impact on our current class structure. This is partly because the social classes on top have numerous advantages, including better education, health, wealth, and connections, which they use to stay on top. Also, as we will study later, discrimination with respect to race and gender has proven very difficult to root out.

As U.S. workers struggled with their lot under monopoly capitalism, a new type of exploitation was underway in less developed countries. More developed and militarily powerful countries in Europe along with the United States and Japan engaged in imperialism.

6.3 THE AGE OF IMPERIALISM

Imperialism, when one country gains control of another country or territory, has happened throughout much of human history. From 1415 to the mid-1800s European powers gained control of the Americas, India, and the coastal areas of Southeast Asia. A second, more rapid wave of imperialism occurred from 1870–1914. Britain, France, Germany, Belgium, and Portugal seized more than 10 million square miles of territory inhabited by more than 180 million people. Almost the entire continent of Africa was part of this seizure. Japan pushed into China and Korea. Meanwhile, the United States seized the Philippines and Cuba and began extending its influence into much of Latin America, dispatching troops to Mexico and countries in the Caribbean 12 times between 1906 and 1929 to shape political and economic structures in a way favorable to the U.S.

This era had important long-term impacts on economic development. Most imperial countries structured their colonies or territories to serve their national interests. Their goals were to obtain cheap raw materials for their industries and to find additional outlets for their manufactured goods. For example, Britain destroyed India's textile industry, forcing India to produce raw cotton instead, which was then exported to Britain at low prices. Britain manufactured the cotton into textiles, which it sold back to India at a substantial profit. In South Africa, Britain seized land from Africans and forced them to work in gold and diamond mines. The result in colony after colony was an underdeveloped economy that produced natural resources but little else. This was extremely deleterious to the development of the colonial economies.

Like Marx, British economist J. A. Hobson saw imperialism as an inevitable product of a capitalist economic system. As technology continued to improve, the industrial economies of the world were producing ever larger quantities of goods. But with workers' wages limited, there often was insufficient demand for all of the products produced: The rich owners could only buy so many things, and low-paid workers could not afford to buy very much. In order to increase profits, companies needed to find lower costs of production, cheaper labor, or new markets in which to sell goods. Colonies offered a potential solution to the problem. Hobson's ideas were later developed and expanded by Vladimir Lenin, the leader of the communist revolution in Russia. By the end of the Age of Imperialism, most of the world had been incorporated into the capitalist economic system, though the colonial economies were structured very differently from those of the industrial powers.

In this world of powerful robber barons, rapidly advancing technology, exploited colonies, a working class in developed economies splintered along racial, ethnic, and gender lines, and ongoing poverty and inequality, mainstream economists attempted to develop a scientific approach to the study of economics building on the ideas of Adam Smith. Their approach was based on a view of markets as competitive, stable, and efficient and of economic actors as rational and calculating (the rational economic man that we studied in Chapter 1).

6.4 THE RISE OF NEOCLASSICAL ECONOMICS

Impressed by the advances in the natural sciences, mainstream economists of the late 1800s attempted to develop a scientific approach to the study of economics. Stanley Jevons, Carl Menger, and Leon Walras developed elegant mathematical models of the economy based on a series of assumptions. They used as the core of their theories some selected ideas of the classical economists (Smith, Say, Ricardo, Malthus) but they incorporated new mathematical approaches, so this approach was labeled "neoclassical" economics. The neoclassical approach forms the basis for modern mainstream economics, and we will study it in much greater detail later in the book. For now, it is worthwhile to sketch out a few key neoclassical ideas to illustrate the difference between this approach and that of Smith, Marx, Veblen, and Keynes.

The possibility of developing a scientific approach to economics is captured by the famous neoclassical economist Alfred Marshall, whose 1890 book, *Principles of Economics*, established the approach still used by many mainstream economists today:

> The raison d'être of economics as a separate science is that it deals chiefly with that part of man's action which is most under the control of measurable motives; and which therefore lends itself better than any other to systematic reasoning and analysis... [W]ith careful precautions money affords a fairly good measure of the moving force of a great part of the motives by which men's lives are fashioned.

If we assume that people behave in a rational and systematic fashion, then we can measure human activity using the dollars that they spend as our guide to understanding their behavior. This, in turn, allows us to construct economic theories and models based on that behavior, and to test our models against actual economic behavior in true scientific fashion.

In the area of consumer theory, neoclassical economists focused on the idea that consumers maximized pleasure or "utility" by selecting rationally from all of the goods available to them, given their tastes, preferences, and income. Similarly, producers maximized profits by using all inputs as efficiently as possible and by selling goods as long as the revenue from selling a good exceeded its cost. Competitive markets also were seen as behaving in a predictable manner according to the neoclassical perspective, with small firms producing goods efficiently at the lowest possible cost and with any excess profits being competed away by the entry of new firms. Thus, the picture of the economy was of a smoothly functioning, stable machine, with everyone making rational, calculated decisions and with free markets providing the best possible outcomes for society, allocating income to the most productive people and producing exactly the amount of goods that people want at the lowest possible price. (To see more examples of the neoclassical approach to economics, look at the model of the production possibilities curve, the supply and demand model, and the model of firm behavior.) Putting this together, *neoclassical economics* focuses on **how rational actors in competitive markets determine incomes and the prices and quantities of goods and services through the interaction of supply and demand.**

At its best, when all of the assumptions of the models hold, neoclassical economics can be extremely useful. When markets are sufficiently competitive we can use the supply and demand model to predict how prices and quantities will change in response to variations in consumer demand,

FIGURE 6.1 Thorstein Veblen (1857–1929).

producer costs, or government policies. This gives us powerful tools to predict how various factors will affect particular markets.

However, some economists found the neoclassical view of the economy to be a far cry from the robber baron capitalism of the late 1800s. Thorstein Veblen, pictured in Figure 6.1, developed an approach to economics that emphasized power structures, culture, and change. Veblen saw little chance of a workers' movement overthrowing capitalism, as Marx had envisioned. Nonetheless, like Smith and Marx before him, Veblen sought to understand the underlying workings of capitalism and, in the process, to develop an economic system that would lead to a fuller unfolding of human life.

6.5 VEBLEN ON EVOLUTION AND INSTITUTIONS

One of the most important aspects of Veblen's analysis was his methodology—his approach to the study of economics. When Veblen looked around him he saw an economic system that was dynamic and constantly changing. Whereas Smith and Marx saw certain "laws" governing how a capitalist economy worked, Veblen saw a world in which the patterns were constantly shifting. To Veblen, anyone who adopted a rigid view of the economy and assumed the future would always work the same as the past was doomed to failure. Instead Veblen adopted an **evolutionary** approach, studying the forces causing the economy to change (or resist change) over time. Veblen believed that economists should analyze the key processes that shape the economy and economic behavior. For example, consumers' behaviors are shaped by biological needs (for food and shelter, procreation, etc.), cultural factors (the need to fit in and succeed in a particular society), industrial factors (competition or the lack of it in various industries, advertising and other media, etc.), government structures (the system of law, regulation, and taxation), and more.

But if the economy is constantly changing and if consumers and firms are constantly buffeted by a variety of factors that affect their behavior, what should economists focus on? To Veblen, the answer was to study *institutions*, which, as noted in Chapter 2, are the organizations, social structures, rules, and habits that structure human interactions and the economy. Once we understand the major institutions in a society, we should have a good grasp of the forces that are promoting and resisting change, which will allow us to analyze the evolution of the economy. The result of Veblen's unique approach was the founding of *institutional economics*, based on the following core ideas: (1) Institutions are the key factors shaping an economy, and should be the primary focus of economists; (2) the economy is constantly changing, and studying how those changes are shaped by technology and key institutions (culture, power structures, and so on) gives us the best possible understanding of the structure of the economic system, how it is evolving, and how it might be improved with effective government policy; and, (3) humans are social beings whose behavior is shaped fundamentally by the institutions of society and who seek status and power based on their cultural values. Implicit in this approach is a critique of neoclassical economics. To Veblen, individual behavior is much less important than studying culture and other institutions that shape human behavior.[3] Utilizing this approach, Veblen made a series of penetrating observations about capitalism, culture, and the "leisure class" that still are relevant today.

6.6 VEBLEN ON CULTURE, PECUNIARY EMULATION, AND CONSPICUOUS CONSUMPTION

In his studies of human societies throughout history, Veblen saw a pattern. In each human society, the members strove to fit in and succeed within the existing cultural norms of that society. As we discussed in Chapter 3, human beings tend to be status-seeking and to act rationally within a cultural context. If, due to a harsh climate or difficult conditions, a society prioritized the sharing of food and resources, people would tend to work cooperatively within that society, seeking status by becoming the most prolific producers of food to share. In a cooperative society, those who were selfish were a threat to the community's survival, and they would be ostracized and shunned, making it less likely that they would survive and reproduce. Survival meant succeeding within the cultural norms of that particular society.

Meanwhile, if a society was more hierarchical, with those on top living ostentatiously and eschewing work while the masses did all of the productive tasks, a different set of cultural values would develop. Overt displays of wealth and leisure came to be valued because they demonstrated that a person was important and of high status in that society. Veblen observed that over time societies with emperors, kings, and nobility came to value outward displays of wealth, such as jewelry, fine clothes, fancy vehicles, and vast estates. They also tended to avoid the type of productive work associated with the common laborers. The elites formed a "leisure class" that sought to develop knowledge of fine wines, food, music, sports, and other cultural markers that showed they had the leisure time to spend on developing these skills instead of work skills. Thus, the leisure class worked very hard at displaying that they did not need to engage in productive work by cultivating useless skills and hobbies!

Veblen saw in all people an **instinct of workmanship**—a desire to work at productive tasks and to achieve something in the process. This too was probably a product of our evolutionary history: Lazy, unmotivated people most likely did not survive. However, in hierarchical societies the fundamentally productive instinct of workmanship in all people became perverted into a vehicle for conspicuous leisure and conspicuous consumption. People worked very hard at acquiring useless goods or skills.

These values of the leisure class were then imitated by the classes below who sought to move up in society, and thus became the values of society as a whole. This is the Veblenian concept of **pecuniary emulation**, where *people from the lower classes imitate the culture, habits, and spending of the upper classes to achieve status for themselves*. This helps us a great deal in understanding how consumption habits in particular societies get established.

Let us consider some specific examples of how human behavior is shaped directly by the culture of the leisure class and how culture evolves over time. Europeans wore cloth around their necks for centuries to use as napkins or to keep their shirts closed in cold weather. However, when King

Louis XIV of France began wearing a fancy lace necktie, or cravat, the necktie became a hot fashion accessory and, eventually, a symbol of status and respect among European nobility. Once the necktie became a symbol of status, it was adopted by businessmen who wanted to improve their social standing. Eventually, wearing a necktie came to symbolize one's seriousness in business and it became a required article of clothing for men at formal occasions in western societies, even when it no longer fulfilled its once-practical purpose as a napkin or neck-warmer. And, this convention spread to other societies around the globe as European countries dominated the global economy during the colonial era. One can find businessmen and government officials wearing neckties in the summer in tropical Africa! Thus, the only way to understand why men in modern societies still purchase and wear neckties is to grasp how the necktie came to symbolize status and respect in the European leisure class in a particular era.

We can see another example in the origins of certain fashion trends for women which developed in the late 1800s when women of status wanted to differentiate themselves from women who worked in factories. Veblen discusses this in his famous book, *The Theory of the Leisure Class*:

> The woman's shoe adds the so-called French heel to the evidence of enforced leisure afforded by its polish; because this high heel obviously makes any, even the simplest and most necessary manual work extremely difficult. The like is true even in a higher degree of the skirt and the rest of the drapery which characterizes woman's dress. The substantial reason for our tenacious attachment to the skirt is just this; it is expensive and it hampers the wearer at every turn and incapacitates her for all useful exertion.[4]

High heels, polished shoes, long hair, long nails, and skirts became signs of status in distinguishing upper-class women from working class women in the U.S. and other industrial societies in the late 1800s. No one could possibly engage in productive work in a factory or on a farm when dressed in this way. Ironically, women's fashions still reflect these trends to a certain degree: Business environments and formal occasions usually are associated with women wearing a skirt and polished shoes with high heels.

Thus, in Veblen's era, those at the top of the pecking order, the "leisure class," displayed that they were too important to work via their "conspicuous consumption" and "conspicuous leisure" patterns. Others then emulated the leisure class, wearing skirts and high heels to work and to important events. This tradition became institutionalized, and it persists to some extent even today, more than a century after it became a cultural norm.

The concept of conspicuous consumption is emblematic of Veblen's sophisticated analysis of how culture and human institutions shape purchasing patterns. **Conspicuous consumption** refers to *the practice of consumers purchasing and using goods for the purposes of displaying their status and importance to others*. All goods have a "use value" or "utility," meaning that they are useful to us and improve our wellbeing. But conspicuous consumption goods also have a "display" or "honorific" value. A good example can be found in the difference between a normal watch such as a Timex and a luxury watch such as a Rolex. Both watches have "use value": They tell us what time it is. But luxury watches also have "display" value. Wearing a Rolex sends a signal to others from our culture that the wearer is a wealthy, important individual. Another obvious example would be the difference between an economy car and a luxury car. Both cars will get the riders to their destination. But only the luxury car will get the rider to their destination in style, impressing others on the way. In both cases, the luxury items send a signal to others from that particular culture that the person who possesses them is important and of high status.

As noted above, the definition of what signifies status varies widely by culture. In ancient tribal societies, everyone knew who the chief was, so it was not as important for the chief to consume conspicuously. In modern, large-scale societies, however, people tend to try to impress others by wearing expensive clothes, jewelry, and watches and driving expensive cars. A fashionably dressed person driving up in a limousine or an expensive car signals that someone important has arrived. Social media today involves substantial conspicuous displays. People attend a concert, for example, to listen to the music. But now that social media is a powerful cultural force, some people spend large amounts of time at concerts taking and posting pictures and videos to their social media accounts. The use value of the event, listening to beautiful music, is only part of the experience. The conspicuous display value of proving that you were at a particularly coveted concert or show is just as important for many people.

Cultural values and consumption patterns do shift over time. In Veblen's era, the elites demonstrated their status via displays of leisure, proving to the world that they were not engaged in productive work via their impractical and impeccable clothing and their knowledge of fine wine and high culture. In the modern U.S., a different value set seems to be emerging. New studies by Neeru Paharia, Silvia Bellezza, and Anat Keinan indicate that in the modern knowledge economy of the U.S., where hard work is prized, people associate busyness with high status.[5] People go out of their way to show and discuss their busy schedules, and this is taken as a sign of how important they are, which indicates a high status in the knowledge sector. Ironically, when the same studies were conducted in Italy the researchers got the opposite results: Participants tended to think those with leisure time were of higher status and those who were busy were of lower status. Thus, the aspiration to be part of the leisure class is still alive and well in Italy!

In these examples, we see that human institutions such as culture have a past-binding, ceremonial aspect that holds onto traditions. However, institutions also have an industrial, technological aspect that promotes change. This dualistic character is readily apparent in the fundamental contrast that often manifests in capitalism between making money and making a useful product that enhances human wellbeing.

6.7 MAKING MONEY VS. MAKING GOODS

Veblen observed a conflict that often existed in capitalist businesses between making money and money goods. The productive aspect of capitalist businesses occurred when they sought to provide a high-quality product that consumers needed at the best possible price. The pursuit of newer technologies to reduce costs and the invention of new, useful products also stemmed from this productive impulse. This side of capitalism was beneficial. Businesses' investments in new technologies after the Civil War ushered in the U.S. Industrial Revolution, developing entirely new industries such as automobiles, telephones, photography, and electricity. These products were often invented by individuals, but it was large-scale businesses engaging in mass production that made these products affordable to the common people.

However, the useful, industrial side of capitalism is often countered by the focus on making money. Businesses could increase profits by eliminating competition or by manipulating consumers via questionable marketing and advertising practices. In the robber baron era, Veblen thought that too much business activity was devoted to wasteful and destructive activities, which he called **industrial sabotage**, and too little was spent on productive efforts. Businesses during the monopoly capitalism era were relentless in colluding (forming "trusts" to fix prices and reduce competition), merging, or using other means to stomp out competition. They bribed or manipulated politicians to get subsidies, prevented foreign competition from entering the market, and kept wages low. In addition to the focus on keeping prices high by reducing competition and wages low by clamping down on workers, companies also engaged in deceptive advertising.

Prior to government regulations, advertising was often misleading or dishonest. Post Foods Company advertised that Grape-Nuts cereal would cure malaria, heart disease, appendicitis, and other maladies, and that it would straighten teeth. Early pharmaceutical companies sold cocaine and opium as elixirs that could cure cancer or as cough remedies, fostering drug addiction in the process. Coca-Cola was developed originally as a "medicine" containing cocaine and caffeine (from kola nuts) that, according to its creator, would cure indigestion, headaches, impotence, and other health problems. These efforts highlight a potentially significant flaw with capitalism: Firms may be able to increase their profits more via manipulative advertising than they can by producing a good product at a low price. This encourages firms to focus on advertising and marketing more than on the product they are producing.

A quick look around the U.S. economy indicates that these opposing forces—making a good product vs. making money—are still a feature of modern capitalism. Each year firms improve old products and invent useful products or new methods for producing existing products for a lower cost. From 2000–2019, firms invented or refined numerous products, including the smart phone and mobile broadband, social media websites, tablets (iPads, Kindles), electric and hybrid cars, GPS navigation systems, robots for surgery and manufacturing, smart devices of all types controlled via voice commands, artificial limbs and medical devices, life-saving drugs, and many more. The ability of capitalist firms to innovate continues unabated.

Unfortunately, there are also many examples of firms prioritizing making money over making a good product. Firms change the styles, colors, packaging or outward design of their products to manipulate consumers into thinking they should purchase the latest versions instead of living with the ones they have. For example, some clothing firms, including Zara and Forever 21, are now churning out new styles every week ("fast fashion") so that consumers keep purchasing new clothes that they do not need in order to stay up with the latest trends. Car companies change models almost every year, so consumers keep buying new models instead of keeping their cars for the normal life span of more than 10 years.

Companies still engage in deceptive or manipulative advertising. Kellogg advertised that Rice Krispies could boost your immune system and Mini-Wheats could make you smarter, making unsubstantiated claims that harken back to the snake oil salesmen of old. Fortunately, we now have laws, enforced by the Federal Trade Commission, that prevent such distortions, and Kellogg was forced to pay fines and compensate consumers for making unsubstantiated health claims.

As a result, most modern advertising is much subtler now, and companies concentrate on manipulating cultural norms and pecuniary emulation to increase sales. Companies sell an image of their product that connects with our cultural values rather than emphasizing the product's practical and useful characteristics. SUV companies show their cars driving up mountains and across rugged terrain, cultivating an image of freedom and adventure even though the vast majority of SUV owners will never drive their vehicle off road. Marketing to teenagers shows people having fun, fitting in, and being "cool" when they buy certain products.

Companies even work hard to reshape cultural norms to sell more stuff. When Miller Lite was developed in the 1970s, the company could not persuade men to buy a "diet" beer which was seen as a product for women. To break through this cultural barrier and reach men, who are the main consumers of beer, Miller started featuring macho men (often professional athletes), often surrounded by beautiful women, in their commercials. Their advertising investment worked, doubling sales and making it socially acceptable for men to drink light beer. This has been so successful that the main beer consumed on many college campuses today is a lite beer such as Natural "Natty" Light, which is the favorite on the campus of Bucknell University where I teach.

In all of these cases, advertisers are playing on the basic human tendency to engage in pecuniary emulation of those who are successful. It is no accident that celebrities are featured prominently in most ads, or that the message of many commercials is that you will appear to be more successful if you buy a particular item.

Similar to the monopoly capitalism era, we also see regular mergers and acquisitions as large firms preserve their dominance of industries by reducing competitive pressures. Apple, Facebook, Amazon, and Google are famous for buying up patents and small companies with new ideas who operate in their markets, in the process ensuring their continued market dominance.

Additionally, firms continue to curry favor with the government. In the U.S., firms and their executives donate vast sums of money to the campaigns of candidates *from both political parties* to ensure that they will receive favorable treatment no matter who wins. If any candidate seems likely to question the status quo, businesses donate huge amounts of money to the competitor. In this way, firms can continue to dominate the economy even if they are not efficiently producing good products. The ability of the dominant powers in a society to resist productive change was one of the worst characteristics of a society to Veblen.

Veblen objected to the domination of the economy by a small group of political and economic elites. Veblen called this group the **vested interests**, because *their goal as the group dominating society is to preserve the status quo that they benefit from*. Their focus is to resist any changes that would displace them from their privileged position atop the social structure. This means preventing new competition in the markets that they dominate via mergers, collusion and threats, and using their power and influence to manipulate the government to do what they want. In Veblen's view, the vested interests tend to impede progress and distort the allocation of resources, preventing the economy from functioning as efficiently as it might otherwise.

Veblen's core ideas—that the economy is structured primarily for the benefit of the few rather than the many, and that it was deeply inefficient due to industrial sabotage, conspicuous consumption, and other wasteful activities—had little influence on the economics profession of his era. Veblen's call to rein in the powers of the vested interests on behalf of the common people went unheeded. As the monopoly capitalist era proceeded, it was subject to vast economic fluctuations, and inequality exploded to levels never before seen in the U.S.

6.8 THE MANUFACTURING BOOM AND THE ROARING 1920S

From 1900–1929, the U.S. economy grew rapidly alongside the rising power and influence of large corporations. The development of electric power drove a huge expansion in manufacturing, which also fed on the large influx of immigrants from Europe and resulted in a significant increase in urbanization. Figure 6.2 shows the dramatic increase in production that occurred in various manufacturing industries. Manufacturing output nearly tripled during this period.

Some of these increases in production were driven by new inventions in manufacturing, in particular, the assembly line. Henry Ford pioneered the assembly line and began making large numbers of the Model T car in 1908. Despite the difficult working conditions, Ford was able to keep his workers by paying them $5 a day, more than twice the going wage rate of $2.25.

Textiles and Apparel	158%
Metals	364%
Steel Products	365%
Paper	420%
Chemicals	483%
Printing and Publishing	500%
Petroleum and Coal	980%
Transportation Equipment	1220%
All Manufacturing	273%

FIGURE 6.2 Increases in manufacturing production, 1899–1929.

Also, with the higher wages his workers were better able to afford the cars that they were producing.

The advent of World War I further stimulated production in the U.S. and cemented the role of the U.S. as the dominant manufacturing power. Following a short recession after the war, the economy boomed with an explosion in mass-produced consumer goods such as cars and appliances. But, the economic growth was extremely uneven and unequal. From 1900–1929, the U.S. experienced 8 recessions, though they were usually short in duration. (The modern U.S. economy typically experiences one recession every 10 years.) During the rapid growth of the Roaring 20s, inequality rose to unprecedented levels. One useful way to measure inequality is to look at the share of national income that goes to the richest 1 percent of the population. Figure 6.2 below shows that, in 1920, the richest 1% of the U.S. population made 14.8% of the country's income. By 1928, that amount had grown to 23.9%.

Inequality can be a major problem for an economy in that it can result in macroeconomic instability. On average, rich people save much more than poor people. When more income goes to those at the top rather than those at the bottom, the result is more savings and less spending on goods. Unless the increase in savings is invested (spent on investment goods such as machines and factories), there will be a shortage of demand (purchases of goods), and the economy will spiral into a recession. Businesses who aren't selling all of their goods lay off workers,

FIGURE 6.3 Income share of the top 1% in the U.S., 1913–2014.

Source: Saez, "Striking it Richer: The Evolution of Top Incomes in the United States," June 25, 2015. https://eml.berkeley.edu/~saez/saez-UStopincomes-2014.pdf.

which reduces incomes further, causing spending to decline even more. What we know from economic history is that the savings of the richest 1% is usually invested in sufficient quantities when investors are confident about that future of the economy, but when investors get spooked for some reason then investment falls below the amount of savings, and the economy enters a recession.

In general, the government of the day took a pro-business, laissez-faire approach. In many locations, the Progressive Movement during this era succeeded in making small changes to the economy for the benefit of workers, such as factory inspections to improve worker treatment and safety; public utilities commissions to limit the pricing of train travel, streetcars, water, and gas; and public health bureaus to address issues of housing, food safety, and disease. At the national level, repeated crises, and especially the Panic of 1907, led to the creation of the Federal Reserve, the U.S. national bank, to control the money and banking system. But the economy remained mostly unregulated until the Great Depression.

6.9 THE GREAT DEPRESSION AND THE FALL OF LAISSEZ-FAIRE

As the economy boomed during the 1920s, very few people recognized the increasingly fragile nature of the economic system. The 1920s saw a doubling of consumer debt, including mortgages for houses as well as installment debt for purchases of cars and appliances. At the same time, investors increasingly bought stocks with borrowed money, called "buying on the margin." Investors were only required to put a 10% down payment on their stock purchases. The increased demand for stocks and the boom of the 1920s caused stock markets to soar. The stock market doubled in 1928 alone! But, a bubble based on debt can pop at any time when investors realize that their investments are not safe.

On October 23, 1929, the stock market started to fall toward the day's end, especially in automobile stocks. As one investor after another panicked, it fell faster and faster, dropping 13% on October 28th and 12% more on October 29th. While there were some temporary recoveries, stock prices continued declining for 3 years, falling a total of 73.4% by 1932.

As the stock prices fell, banks started failing. People who borrowed money to invest in the stock market could not pay back their loans, and banks started to run out of money. When a few banks had lost so much that they were unable to give depositors their money when they wanted to withdraw it, depositors panicked. Even those depositors whose money was in stable banks decided to withdraw all of their deposits rather than worry that they might lose their money like other depositors at other banks had. The result was a "run on the bank," where banks, who had loaned out most of the money of their depositors, could not meet the demands for cash withdrawals. By 1933, 11,000 of the country's 25,000 banks had failed. There was no federal deposit insurance yet, so when banks failed the depositors lost their money. This resulted in a significant decline in the U.S. money supply and an increase in the real interest rate of more than 10% as money became scarce.

These events were devastating to the economy. As people saw their life savings evaporate in the stock market or in failed banks, they cut back on spending. Businesses saw their sales plummet, so they laid off workers and cut investment. This reduced incomes, causing even more decreases in spending, and more layoffs and declines in investment. The decline in consumer demand caused prices for farmers to plunge, driving thousands bankrupt. More than 85,000 businesses closed, and unemployment reached an astounding 25%. Unemployment insurance and welfare programs did not exist at the time, so people became desperate. Some starved, while others depended on charities, begging, or picking through garbage dumps for food. U.S. National Income fell from $87 billion in 1929 to $42 billion in 1932, and kept falling. The U.S. economy was the largest in the world, and it was closely tied with Europe, so the contagion quickly spread to Europe and then the rest of the world. Soon the entire world was in a depression.

U.S. President Herbert Hoover, and most economists of the day, thought that the depression would pass as quickly as others had. Hoover refused to take dramatic action, arguing that involving the government in the economy would be akin to socialism. Meanwhile, the neoclassical economists of the day kept arguing that the economy would return to equilibrium in the "long run," which would happen very soon. Hoover and his economic advisors also pushed austerity (see Chapter 1). Believing that a balanced government budget was necessary, they slashed spending and enacted the largest tax increase in history (for that time) in 1932, throwing even more people out of work, all in the belief that the depression would soon disappear. The response of the great macroeconomist John Maynard Keynes to this type of argument was a devastating critique of this approach. Keynes said, "The long run is a misleading guide to current affairs. *In the long run we are all dead*. Economists set themselves too easy, too useless a task if in tempestuous seasons they can only tell us that when the storm is past the ocean is flat again."[6] To Keynes it was ridiculous to wait for the long run equilibrium, which might take years to come, when we have the tools to end the depression much sooner.

Franklin Delano Roosevelt was elected president in 1932 by promising a "New Deal" for Americans in which the government would get much more directly involved in the economy, regulating huge firms, creating jobs, and providing a safety net for workers. Drawing on the ideas of Thorstein Veblen's students and, especially, John Maynard Keynes, Roosevelt ushered in the modern era of the mixed economy in which the core economic system is still capitalist, but the government takes on a significant role in regulating and stabilizing the economy. The era of laissez-faire capitalism had come to an end, destroyed by the Great Depression and the Keynesian Revolution.

6.10 CONCLUSION

The period from the mid-1800s to 1932 was a tumultuous one for the United States. After the Civil War, the manufacturing sector in the U.S. exploded, driven first by government-led investment in railroads, and later by huge, monopolistic corporations and trusts. The first attempts to regulate corporations were undertaken as the Progressive Movement grew, but, in general, the government took a pro-business, laissez-faire approach to regulation. Despite the rapid rate of growth, there were warning signs in the frequent crises and rising inequality of the period.

Neoclassical economists of this era devoted their energies to developing a mathematical approach to the discipline that would be rigorous, logical, and scientific. They constructed elaborate models of consumer and producer behavior based on assumptions that all markets were efficient and competitive, and all consumers and firms were rational actors motivated by money. This allowed neoclassical economists to make predictions regarding economic behavior. However, the assumption that all markets would reach equilibrium in the long run became increasingly untenable as the Great Depression grew longer and longer, with markets staying in disequilibrium for years at a time.

Meanwhile, Thorstein Veblen was developing the evolutionary, institutionalist approach to economics, bringing anthropology and psychology into his analysis to understand human behavior. He observed the status-seeking behavior common to human societies and noted how conspicuous consumption and conspicuous leisure had become the markers of respectability in the U.S., demonstrating to the outside world the status and importance of a person.

Recent trends in economics demonstrate the ongoing importance of Veblen's methodology. Mainstream economists have increasingly been incorporating institutions into their analysis. Marxian economists have moved away from deterministic attitudes toward capitalism to a more evolutionary perspective. Thus, Veblen's contributions to the field are significant and enduring, as are those of John Maynard Keynes, whose ideas we take up next.

QUESTIONS FOR REVIEW

1. How was the era of monopoly capitalism different from the competitive capitalism of Adam Smith's era? Does Smith's argument that unregulated capitalism will tend to benefit the workers hold up under monopoly capitalism?

2. How do race and gender interact with social class to affect opportunities?

3. How did the Age of Imperialism restructure the global economic system?

4. Describe how Veblen's "evolutionary" approach to economics differs from the approaches of Smith, Marx, and neoclassical economics.

5. Describe the role of the leisure class, conspicuous consumption, and pecuniary emulation in the economy. Apply the concepts of conspicuous consumption and pecuniary emulation to the modern world, including examples from your community or university.

6. Define what Veblen means by conspicuous consumption. Make a list of at least 3 items that people in your community or university seem to purchase more for the purposes of conspicuous consumption than for the usefulness of the item. Briefly explain why you chose these particular items. Do not use examples already given in this book.

7. Why does Veblen distinguish between making money (via industrial sabotage) vs. making goods? Explain briefly.

8. Why does Veblen think that culture is important in understanding human behavior? Explain.

9. How did the "Roaring '20s" set the stage for the Great Depression? How did the Great Depression create the conditions for the Keynesian Revolution in economics?

10. Veblen focused on institutions and how those institutions tend to persist over time, largely due to the forces of culture and the power of the vested interests to resist change. But, these institutions also evolve. Using Veblen's approach, analyze the persistence and evolution of one of the following factors over time: (a) Racial inequality, (b) gender inequality, (c) class inequality, (d) domination of the economy by large corporations, or (e) domination of the global economy by the former imperial powers.

NOTES

1. Howard Zinn, *A People's History of the United States*, Abridged Teaching Edition, 2003, p. 190.

2. *Ibid.*, p. 33.

3. See Geoffrey M. Hodgson, "What Is the Essence of Institutional Economics," *Journal of Economic Issues*, 34, 2 (June 2000), pp. 317–329, for a broader description of institutional economics.

4. Thorstein Veblen (1899), *The Theory of the Leisure Class*, Dover, Reprinted 1994, p. 105.

5. Bellezza, Silvia, Neeru Paharia and Anat Keinan, "Research: Why Americans Are So Impressed by Busyness," *Harvard Business Review*, December 15, 2016, https://hbr.org/2016/12/research-why-americans-are-so-impressed-by-busyness, accessed July 29, 2017.

6. John Maynard Keynes, *A Tract on Monetary Reform* (1923), ch. 3, p. 80.

Keynes and mixed market capitalism

How to save capitalism from itself

In the U.S. and Europe, a new role for government inspired by the ideas of Thorstein Veblen and John Maynard Keynes emerged, aiming to reduce the worst excesses of markets while still preserving the best aspects of market capitalism—competition, innovation, and economic growth. Followers of Veblen and Keynes worked in the U.S. government to establish stabilization policies, unemployment insurance, Social Security, and other programs to create a safety net for all citizens and to legalize labor unions.

Keynes revolutionized economic thinking by establishing the field of **macroeconomics,** which is **the study of the aggregate forces that shape national economies.** Macroeconomics studies large-scale, aggregate patterns in spending, saving, and investment, and how these patterns create the *business cycle*—**the pattern of booms and busts created by economic fluctuations in market capitalist economies.** Keynes demonstrated that aggregate forces at the national and international level have fundamentally different dynamics than microeconomic markets. National economies, and especially financial markets, are subject to "animal spirits" that spark booms and busts, rendering the economy unstable at times. Keynes advocated stabilization policy, to smooth out the business cycle, reduce the severity of recessions, and create a more sound economic system. In this way, Keynes sought to save capitalism from the destructive forces within it.

As governments began implementing Keynesian policies and regulating markets, the result was the modern, mixed economy consisting of some government and some market influence. Mixed market capitalism proved to be a relatively stable and robust system, generating rapid economic growth and a much less unequal distribution of the gains from capitalism.

Friedrich Hayek criticized this growth of government's role, worrying that it would lead to totalitarianism of the kind seen in Nazi Germany and the Soviet Union. Despite Hayek's cautions, most Western democracies adopted mixed market capitalism, though with varying degrees of government intervention and varying degrees of success. However, the oil shocks of the 1970s, and the era of globalization and environmental crisis that followed, exposed some of the main contradictions in mixed market capitalism.

This chapter begins by describing the economic theories that led neoclassical economists to advocate a laissez-faire, hands-off approach to the economy even in the depths of the Great Depression. Next, we take up the ideas of John Maynard Keynes in more detail, describing his critique of neoclassical economics of his day, and his major ideas regarding the circular flow of the economy, leakages and injections, the multiplier, sticky wages, and other market rigidities. Subsequently, we discuss the New Deal and the government policies that were established in the U.S. and elsewhere to stabilize economies and end the Great Depression. We then turn briefly to the ideas of Friedrich Hayek, and his critique of Keynesian policies and central planning. The chapter concludes by looking at the mixed market economy that developed in the U.S. after the New Deal and that still exists today.

7.0 CHAPTER 7 LEARNING GOALS

After reading this chapter you should be able to:

- List, explain and evaluate the 3 core theoretical ideas that drove neoclassical economists of the early 1900s to advocate a hands-off, laissez-faire approach to the economy: The Marginal Productivity Theory of Distribution, Markets Always Clear, and Say's Law;
- Reproduce the circular flow model of the economy and use it to explain how neoclassical economists and Keynes differ in their analysis of savings and investment (leakages and injections);
- List, explain, and evaluate the major ideas of John Maynard Keynes, including the volatility of investment, sticky wages and prices, the macroeconomic problems created by wage and price deflation, the multiplier process, and stabilization policy;
- Compare and contrast the ideas of Hayek and Austrian economists with those Keynes;

- Describe and analyze the economic interventions made by the U.S. government from the New Deal to the present;
- Define and evaluate the effectiveness of an economic system of "regulated" or "mixed" market capitalism.

7.1 NEOCLASSICAL ECONOMICS AND THE IDEOLOGY OF LAISSEZ-FAIRE

The neoclassical economists of the early 1900s held 3 theoretical beliefs that led most of them to conclude that a laissez-faire approach to economic regulation was always preferable to government intervention. These theories were the Marginal Productivity Theory of Distribution, Markets Always Clear (supply equals demand, along with the "invisible hand"), and Say's Law. We take each of these up below.

1. The *Marginal Productivity Theory of Distribution*: The neoclassical theory that people are paid exactly what they are worth based on their marginal productivity under a competitive, capitalist economic system. This theory assumes that there are no power imbalances, so no exploitative relationships exist.

   The implications of this theory are important to understand. Since all markets are assumed to be fully competitive, workers should always have multiple employers trying to hire them, and employers should always have multiple workers to choose from. In essence, workers are assumed to have as much bargaining power as their bosses. Under such conditions, a worker will end up getting paid exactly what they are worth based on how productive they are. If a worker is particularly productive (a high marginal productivity), many employers will bid for their services and their wages will be high. If a worker is less productive (a low marginal productivity), they will be paid a lower wage in a competitive marketplace. Also, another assumption behind this theory was that everyone had equal access to education and opportunities, so it did not matter if someone was well-connected. If this theory holds true then the government should never take steps to reduce inequality, because that would mean taking money from highly productive people and giving it to less productive people, reducing the efficiency of the economy. Thus, despite the exploding inequality of the 1920s, no efforts were made to equalize incomes.

2. *Markets Always Clear*: The neoclassical theory that supply always equals demand in all markets, so the invisible hand of the market always allocates resources efficiently.

If all markets are competitive and there is easy entry and exit of firms, then prices will always adjust to eliminate any surplus or shortage. If there is a glut of goods produced, then the prices of those goods will fall, causing consumers to buy more and eliminating the glut. So, the surplus of goods in a depression will be eliminated once prices of goods fall, which causes consumers to buy more of them. If there is unemployment, otherwise known as a surplus of laborers, unemployment will disappear as soon as wages fall because then firms will hire more workers and the surplus will be eliminated. According to this theory, the only possible reason for unemployment was if workers demanded higher wages than they were entitled to. Edwin Cannan, President of the Royal Economic Society in England, put it this way in 1932: "General unemployment appears when asking too much is a general phenomenon... [T]he world ... should learn to submit to declines of money-incomes without squealing."[1] Neoclassical economists saw no need to intervene in the economy to help the unemployed or producers. Any government intervention was seen as reducing the efficiency of the market mechanism: Capitalist markets were seen as the ideal, rational, and efficient way to allocate society's resources.

3. *Say's Law*: **Supply creates its own demand, and savings is always equal to investment**.

As we saw in Chapter 4, Say's Law posits that in the act of supplying products firms generate income. Since every penny a firm earns in revenue is income for someone—either the workers, suppliers, or owners—there is always enough income generated to purchase all of the goods produced. Also, any amount of income that people save will automatically be invested. When people save money, they put it in banks. The banks need to loan that money out to make a profit, so they offer loans at favorable interest rates. Businesses looking to expand their operations and consumers desiring more goods borrow from banks, and when they spend the money they borrowed the money in banks has been returned to the economy and the circular flow is complete. Any time there is a decline in spending and an increase in savings, perhaps because consumers are pessimistic after a stock market crash, there will be a larger amount of money in banks, which in turn causes the banks to reduce interest rates, which then stimulates investment and consumption spending, eliminating any problems created by the original decline in spending. There is always exactly enough demand to buy all the goods that are supplied. This is the famous "Circular Flow Model of the Economy," depicted in Figure 7.1.

Recall that in the circular flow model firms produce goods and services, which they sell to consumers and to other businesses (businesses

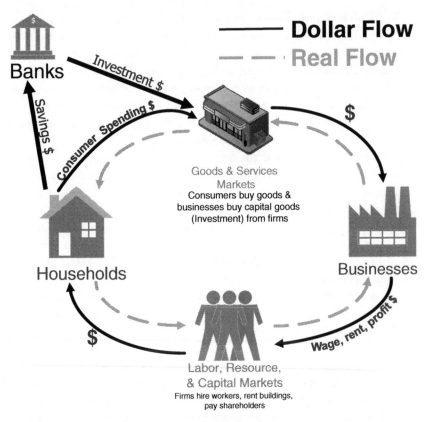

FIGURE 7.1 The circular flow model of the economy, with savings and investment.

purchase capital goods, such as machinery and equipment). Every dollar of income that the producers generate when they sell goods and services becomes income for somebody: Firms pay wages to workers hired in labor markets, they pay rent on land to landowners in real estate markets, and they pay interest to banks, dividends to shareholders, and profits to owners in capital (financial) markets. What do households do with the income they earn? They either spend it, in the form of consumer spending on goods and services, or they save it, putting their money in banks. The money placed in banks is then loaned out to businesses for purchases of capital goods or to consumers for the purchase of consumer durables (houses, cars, and appliances), putting the money back into the economy. Note that businesses' purchases of capital goods and consumer purchases of durable goods are considered to by physical investment. According to Say's Law, all the money that is taken out of the economy in the form of savings is put back into the economy in the form of investment.

7.2 THE MACROECONOMIC REVOLUTION OF JOHN MAYNARD KEYNES

John Maynard Keynes (1883–1946), pictured in Figure 7.2,[2] was born in Cambridge, England. His father was a well-known economist, and he studied with the famous neoclassical economist Alfred Marshall at Cambridge. Even early in his career, he demonstrated extraordinary sophistication and foresight in his analysis. In his famous book, *The Economic Consequences of the Peace* (1919), he predicted that the harsh financial conditions imposed on Germany after World War I, requiring it to pay more than 80% of GDP in reparations, would cause impoverishment and starvation and would eventually lead to another war even worse than World War I. The German hyperinflation and crisis of the 1920s, followed by the rise of Adolf Hitler and Nazi Germany, and the advent of World War II in 1939, showed just how accurate Keynes' predictions were. He was also able to use his knowledge of the economy to make a fortune for himself and for King's College in financial markets.

Rather than depending on abstract, deductive theory based on questionable assumptions, Keynes based his ideas on observations of actual

FIGURE 7.2 J.M. Keynes (1883–1946).

investor and worker behavior. What he saw was a picture very different from the one described in the neoclassical theories of the day.

The first major flaw in neoclassical analysis, according to Keynes, was with Say's Law. As you can see with the circular flow model above, Say's Law only holds if savings and other leakages out of the economy are equal to investment and other injections into the economy. (Later, we will include additional leakages such as export spending and taxes, and additional injections such as import spending and government spending.) However, Keynes observed that when a crisis hits, savings increases but investment falls as businesses lose confidence, leakages then exceed injections, and the economy spirals into a recession. Thus, the first pillar of Keynesian analysis is the inherent *volatility of investment*.

1. *Volatility of investment*: **The Keynesian theory that business purchases of capital goods (investment) depend primarily on expected future profits, which are driven largely by expected sales, and expectations can vary dramatically.** When businesses' expectations change, we can anticipate large changes in investment, resulting in the booms and busts of the business cycle.

Say's Law fails precisely because it does not incorporate this fundamental driver of investor behavior. The stock market crash of 1929 and failures of banks undermined business confidence and reduced consumer spending as people saw their wealth decline. According to Say's Law, the decrease in spending meant that people were saving more, and more money in banks should have led to lower interest rates which should have prompted more investment. But few businesses were investing despite lower interest rates. Why? Because expected sales were very low. With consumer spending down and unemployment spiraling out of control, no sane businessperson would see 1932 as a good time to increase investment.

Recall that investment, the purchase of capital goods, usually increases the size and scale of business operations. Businesses will not invest unless they expect to sell more goods in the future. The main reason for this is that it can take a long time, often more than a year, for a business investment to start earning profits. A business that builds a new factory must lay out large sums of money now for a plant that could take 2 years before it has been built, staffed, and become operational. When it invests, the business is making a bet that it can sell more goods in 2 years than it does now. The only conditions under which the business will make the investment in the new factory is if it expects sales to be very good in 2 years. A pessimistic sales forecast would likely mean the business will not undertake the investment. This is why business expectations are such an important driver of investment, which is an important driver of the business cycle.

In the Great Depression, as unemployment increased and consumer spending fell, businesses cut their investment even though interest rates were low. Thus, there was no increase in investment forthcoming, as Say's law had predicted, and the economy languished in the Great Depression for years. Savings continued to exceed investment. This problem was exacerbated when banks failed, reducing the money supply and causing interest rates to increase. Furthermore, the unemployment rate failed to decrease, as the neoclassical economists had predicted. One of the main causes of this was sticky wages.

2. *Sticky wages and prices*: Keynes' observed that, **in a recession, wages and prices do not fall fast enough to encourage businesses to hire more workers and consumers to buy more goods.**

What Keynes found was that it took a very long time after the start of a recession for wages to fall. Workers and their unions fought any wage cuts vigorously and angrily, so slashing wages often meant strikes and lower productivity, which were bad for profits. However, employers have found that if they keep wages the same and lay off some of their work force, the results are different. Workers who keep their jobs in the face of layoffs are very happy to have them. They will work harder and more productively to keep their jobs so that they do not get laid off in the future. In this sense, wages are "sticky downward": They tend to increase in booms when the unemployment rate falls and workers are in demand, but wages tend to stay the same for a long time in recessions before falling eventually if the recession persists for several years.

For example, Leo Wolman of the National Bureau of Economic Research reported that after the stock market crash in 1929, real wages fell very little in 1930 and 1931, and only fell in 1932 in non-union and non-utilities industries.[3] Meanwhile, unemployment surged. So 3 years after the crash, the Great Depression persisted with large increases in layoffs but only small declines in wages in some sectors. Wages did not fall far enough and fast enough to spark a rise in employment that would have helped to end the Great Depression, as neoclassical economic theory implied. But, even where wages did fall, there was not the desired increase in employment that neoclassical economic theory had predicted, as we will see below.

The story with prices is a bit different. Prices of goods did not fall significantly for the first 6 months after the stock market crash, but then they began to fall quickly. As the economy crashed, surpluses of goods began to pile up because no one was buying them, and that caused prices to fall in one market after another. Prices fell by more than 20% from 1930–1933. According to the neoclassical theory of the day, that decline in prices should have sparked an increase in consumer purchases, helping to solve the Depression. Instead, deflation and declines in wages proved to be ruinous.

3. *Macroeconomic problems created by wage and price deflation*: **Declines in wages undermine aggregate demand and declines in goods' prices undermine business profitability, both of which harm the economy in particular ways.**

One of the important economic facts that Keynes established was that, in general, wage declines are bad for economic growth. Neoclassical economic theory of the time predicted that a decline in wages, by reducing the cost of hiring, would cause employers to hire more workers and boost the economy. However, neoclassical economists were only focusing on the cost, or supply, side of the wage issue, ignoring the demand side. When wages fall, workers have less money to spend. When workers spend less, sales fall at businesses, who then lay off workers due to poor sales. Thus, when wages decline, the total demand for goods and services (aggregate demand) falls, which prevents employment from increasing (despite the decrease in wage costs) and harms real GDP growth.

Declines in prices are also destructive to economic growth. In fact, deflation is one of the worst things that can happen to a business. Imagine Henry Ford producing 1 million basic Model A cars for an average cost of $450 in 1930, and being able to sell them for $500 to make a reasonable profit. But, with deflation, if the price at which he can sell the Model A car falls 11 percent, to $445, then he takes a loss on every car he sells. Losses, if they continue, will result eventually in bankruptcy. By reducing the prices that businesses can sell their goods to below what it costs to produce, deflation can be ruinous to producers.

As a classic example from the Depression, the price of milk fell so low that farmers lost money on each gallon they sold. In desperation, the farmers went on strike, dumping their milk and blocking milk shipments of non-striking farmers to try to boost prices and call attention to their plight. Similar dumping and destruction of food happened with oranges, potatoes, pigs, and other farm products. It is remarkable to think of children dying of malnutrition at the same time that food was being destroyed due to low prices, something John Steinbeck called "a crime ... that goes beyond denunciation" in his famous novel about the Depression, *The Grapes of Wrath*. Deflation was one of the most devastating aspects of the Depression, and it remains a significant problem for economies in recessions. It also is important to understand how the contagion of a downturn spreads from one sector to another via the multiplier process.

4. *Multiplier process*: A respending process whereby a dollar in spending becomes income for someone else, which they then spend, which becomes additional income, and so on, so that a dollar of spending is respent multiple times. Similarly, when a firm lays off workers and incomes decline, those workers spend less, which reduces incomes at the businesses they usually patronize, which lowers revenues of those businesses, which causes them to lay off workers who then spend less, which lowers incomes more, which lowers spending more, and so on.

The stock market crash of 1929 caused businesses to cancel investment projects such as the building of new factories, and it caused consumers to cut their spending on expensive, durable goods such as houses, cars, and appliances. These declines in spending reduced the incomes of firms in the construction and durable goods sectors. Those firms, in turn, laid off workers and cut their investment spending. When the workers in construction and durable goods lost their jobs, they too cut their spending, buying fewer goods of all types, which hurt those businesses that they usually patronized. And on and on it went. Thus, one major macroeconomic event, like a stock market crash, can spread like a contagion to other parts of the economy. Fortunately, Keynes observed, crashes can be reversed if the government will engage in appropriate stabilization policy.

Taken together, these key Keynesian insights tell us that there is no reason to expect recessions to fix themselves. Given that the economy can linger in a recession for long periods of time, as it did in the Great Depression, Keynes argued that in recessions the government should use all of the tools at their disposal to stimulate the economy. This "stabilization policy" meant abandoning the laissez-faire approach and actively using government policy to improve the economy.

7.3 MACROECONOMIC STABILIZATION POLICY

As we noted in the previous chapter, Keynes thought it was ridiculous to wait for the economy to eventually improve, stating sarcastically, "In the long run we are all dead." Instead, he advocated taking concrete, immediate government action to stimulate the economy. He thought the government should engage in macroeconomic *stabilization policy*: (1) Increase government spending, (2) reduce taxes, and (3) reduce interest rates in recessions, while doing the opposite when the economy is growing too quickly.

Increasing government spending was the surest way to improve economic conditions in a recession. The biggest problem in a recession was that there was too little spending (a shortage of aggregate demand): Investors and consumers weren't buying enough goods to keep the economy going at its normal rate. Therefore, the best way to correct the economy was for the government to increase spending because this would directly increase incomes and then, via the multiplier, spark additional rounds of spending. If the government were to spend billions of dollars building roads, bridges, parks, and schools, it would create jobs and income for millions of workers necessary to build those things. Those workers would then spend the income they received, further stimulating the economy.

The government could also cut taxes, giving consumers and businesses more money to spend. As they spend more, this will stimulate income and job growth. Tax cuts should be targeted at poor and middle-class families, who will spend the largest percentage of their tax cut and therefore stimulate spending the most. However, tax cuts tend to be less effective than government spending in recessions because of poor consumer and business confidence. If consumers are pessimistic about the future, worrying that they might lose their job or fall on hard times, then they will likely save the tax cut instead of spending it. Similarly, businesses who get a tax cut in a recession might use that money to invest in new plants and equipment, but if they expect slow sales to continue, they too might save the money from the tax cut instead of spending it. Tax cuts tend to be less effective than government spending in a recession because some (and possibly a lot) of the tax cut will be saved whereas all of the government project money is spent.

The government should also increase the money supply in order to reduce interest rates in a recession. As the government floods the banking system with money, banks will seek to loan out the new money to new borrowers, which will require them to lower interest rates to entice new borrowers. One of the major problems in the Great Depression was that when banks failed, this significantly reduced the money supply and increased real interest rates, which made businesses and consumers reluctant to borrow for spending on investment and consumer durable goods. Increasing the money supply would help to reverse that problem.

Unfortunately, like tax cuts, declines in interest rates can have limited effectiveness in a recession due to pessimism. Consumers might not be willing to borrow more money for new houses and cars if they are worried about keeping their job in the future. And employers might not be willing to borrow money to finance new investment purchases of plants and equipment if they expected slow sales to continue in the future. There is no guarantee that lowering interest rates will spark significant increases in investment and consumer spending.

The best possible way to combat a recession would be to enact all 3 policies, increasing spending, reducing taxes, and reducing interest rates so that every possible lever is used to stimulate the economy. In fact, the government did all of these things to combat the Great Recession of 2008–2009. Note that enacting stabilization policy not only requires the government to intervene in the economy, it also requires that the government run a deficit and borrow money in a recession. Running deficits, however, was the opposite of the policy of austerity recommended by most neoclassical economists of the day.

As we noted in Chapter 1, government deficits tend to increase automatically in recessions, and this was particularly true during the Great Depression. As incomes and spending fell after the stock market crash, tax revenues fell as well, creating budget deficits for the government now that tax revenues were below spending. Neoclassical economists argued that the government should increase taxes and cut government spending to balance the budget. But in cases where the government did this, the recession worsened. Increases in taxes reduced spending, as did cuts in government programs. Keynes suggested the opposite. Even though the budget deficit has increased in a recession, the government should run even larger deficits by cutting taxes and increasing spending. Those policies will increase income and stimulate economic growth, which will then increase tax revenues in the future. In essence, running government deficits during recessions pays for itself once economic growth returns.

Here, Keynes argued for a revolution in thinking about government intervention and government budgets. Instead of running a balanced budget each and every year, governments should run deficits in recessions, which could then be paid off by surpluses that are run during expansions when economic growth is more rapid and incomes (and tax revenues) are higher. The government budget should be balanced over the entire business cycle, not each year. Governments must have the flexibility to run deficits when conditions are bad, and to slow down the economy by running a surplus when they see the economy growing too quickly—an overheated economy—which can lead to a bubble and a crash.

7.4 THE NEW DEAL AND THE RISE OF THE MIXED ECONOMY

In the 1932 U.S. campaign for president, Franklin Delano Roosevelt promised to stop following a laissez-faire approach and to take direct government action to end the Great Depression, adopting a philosophy similar to Keynes called the "New Deal." He won the election in a landslide over Herbert Hoover, winning by 18 percentage points and bringing a Democratic Congress into office with him. After inauguration in 1933, Roosevelt and Congress enacted 15 major bills in the first 100 days to begin to transform the U.S. into a mixed market economy. Over the next two years, even more changes were made. The major areas of reform were: (1) Regulation of banking, financial markets, and the money supply; (2) the creation of a safety net for people who had fallen on hard times; (3) the direct provision of jobs for the unemployed; (4) the establishment of the Social Security retirement program for the elderly; and (5) the creation of an agricultural price support system.

Regulation of banking, money, and financial markets

One of the major problems after the stock market crash had been bank failures. Consumers and businesses lost their savings when the banks failed, which made everyone reluctant to put their money into banks once they had some. Many people hid cash under their mattresses rather than entrust their money to a bank! But, the lack of savings in banks was very bad for the economy. There was little money for businesses and consumers to borrow, which stifled business investment and consumer purchases of houses, cars, and appliances.

To solve this problem, the Roosevelt administration created Federal Deposit Insurance, where the government would guarantee deposits of up to $5000 per individual in banks (that amount has grown to $250,000 per individual today). This means that if the bank fails, the government would reimburse depositors for any money the bank lost. In exchange for providing this insurance, the government imposed strict regulations on banks. Insured banks were prohibited from engaging in speculative investments in the stock market, they had to agree to keep a certain amount of cash on hand (reserves) to prevent runs on the bank, and they were required to submit to regular inspections from bank regulators. The government split the banking sector into safe, insured mortgage banks and riskier, non-insured investment banks. The government also established itself as the "lender of last resort," meaning that if a bank ran short of cash it could borrow from the Fed. And, it established the possibility of the federal government seizing insolvent banks and bailing out banks experiencing financial difficulty.

Investment banks and stock markets were now to be regulated by the newly created Securities and Exchange Commission. The SEC established rules and guidelines for financial markets, mandated transparency, and outlawed insider trading and other unethical market manipulations.

The government also took greater control of the money supply—which at the time meant controlling the supply of gold and the issuance of Federal Bank notes backed by gold. By devaluing the dollar relative to gold (and also relative to other currencies backed by gold), the money supply increased. By flooding banks with money, real interest rates dropped as banks sought to find new borrowers, stimulating investment and consumer spending. Devaluing the dollar relative to other currencies also increased U.S. exports because it made U.S. goods cheaper to foreign consumers.

Together, the banking, financial market, and money supply reforms restored faith in the financial system. People began putting their savings in banks and stock markets once again, the money supply expanded significantly, real interest rates fell, and consumer spending and business investment started to increase. Ironically, although many of these reforms were looked at as "socialism" by those opposing government intervention, they were proposed and enacted by conservative bankers who saw these changes as the only way to save capitalism.

The safety net: Social Security, unemployment insurance, and welfare

In addition to its path-breaking regulation of banks, financial markets, and the money supply, the New Deal established a "safety net" for those who fell on hard times with the Social Security Act. This too was a revolutionary change in philosophy, with the government for the first time taking on the role of insuring that its citizens "fared well," in what came to be termed the "welfare state." The first key component of the new welfare state was the Social Security program.

In the 1930s, the elderly were among the poorest segments of the population. Most workers in that era did not receive pensions, there was no government-provided old age insurance, the jobs that did exist in the Depression went to younger workers, and many of the elderly had lost their life savings in the bank failures of the early 1930s. To rectify this situation, the Roosevelt administration established the Social Security program as a national system of old age insurance. Once workers reached age 65, they would receive a payment from the government based on the amount they had earned during their lifetime, up to a limit. In order to start the program immediately to address the poverty of the elderly, the Social Security program was established as a pay-as-you-go system: Workers and employers in the 1930s would pay a Social Security tax which would go directly to existing retirees. When those workers and employers retired, say in the 1950s, their Social Security benefits would be paid out of taxes from new workers and employers. There are no retirement accounts within the U.S. Social Security system. Rather, by working in the U.S., you acquire the right to a certain amount of Social Security retirement benefits, which will be paid as long as there are enough workers and employers paying Social Security taxes to support you and other retirees.

Another major innovation of the Social Security Act was the establishment of unemployment insurance. This program provides temporary assistance, usually for up to 6 months, to a worker after she or he loses their job.

(In recent recessions the government has regularly extended unemployment benefits beyond 6 months when conditions are such that unemployed workers have little chance of finding a job.)

Workers who were unable to find jobs or generate income for prolonged periods of time and who became destitute would qualify for welfare programs, designed to help the poorest, most desperate people in society. These programs also helped to support single mothers and their children and the disabled. During the Depression, since many families were no longer able to support their relatives who had fallen on hard times, the government increasingly took on this role.

Intervention in the labor market: Job creation and labor laws

Due to the massive nature of the unemployment problem, Roosevelt also created new programs to put people back to work directly. The Civilian Conservation Corps employed hundreds of thousands of unemployed, unmarried men between the ages of 17 and 27. These men planted more than 3 billion trees to stop land erosion and beautify towns. The Civil Works Administration, the National Industrial Recovery Act, and the Works Progress Administration employed people to build roads, schools, national parks, and airports, or to serve as teachers. Until the U.S. entered World War II, these programs employed more than 15 million people at various times on a variety of public works projects. The efforts were so successful at job creation and achieved so many useful things in communities that some reformers began to consider the idea that the government should be the "employer of last resort" in recessions, employing people who wanted to work but could not find a job.

Other dramatic actions were taken in labor markets as well. The government legalized the right of workers to unionize and the right of unions to collectively bargain with employers. **Collective bargaining occurs when workers bargain as a group (union) with employers instead of each worker bargaining separately with an employer.** This significantly strengthens the bargaining power of employees, allowing them to get better wages and benefits and greater job security. When employees bargain on their own with their employer, they have little power in negotiations. When the workers bargain as a group, they can threaten to go on strike and shut down the entire company if their demands are not met, giving them much more say in pay and working conditions. The government also established minimum wages in many industries, reduced the standard work week to 40 hours, and abolished child labor. In addition to these interventions in labor markets, the government also began regulating agricultural markets.

Agricultural price supports

Farmers were among the groups hardest hit by the Depression, when agricultural prices plummeted in the early 1930s. To alleviate the farmers' plight, Roosevelt paid them to produce less, reducing the supply of agricultural products so that prices would increase and farmers would make more money. Although this policy was condemned by many given that there were a lot of hungry people in the U.S. at the time, it succeeded in stabilizing agricultural markets.

The success of the New Deal

The New Deal reforms had a very positive effect on the economy, finally ending the freefall that began in 1929. Financial markets and banks were stabilized by the reforms. Unemployment insurance, welfare, job creation, and Social Security programs directly put money into the hands of poor households, and they spent it, stimulating aggregate demand, increasing businesses' sales, and sparking even more hiring. From 1933–1937, business investment increased by more than 1200%, consumer spending increased by more than 46%, and Real GDP had returned to its 1929 level.

In general, the New Deal was pragmatic and modest in scope, intending to stabilize markets and to correct market failures where they were most glaring—especially in labor, finance, banking and agriculture. Despite these modest goals, it ushered in a new era of government intervention in the economy, with the state assuming the role of stabilizer of markets and insurer of the welfare of its citizens. Nonetheless, many people were worried about this unprecedented increase in the government's role and especially the 83% increase in government spending.

The Recession of 1937–1938

Despite all the successes of the New Deal and the positive growth that had been achieved, the Roosevelt administration still had not completely embraced Keynesian economics and the need to run substantial deficits and engage in expansionary monetary policy until the economy had fully recovered. Business investment was still 27 percent lower in 1937 than it had been in 1929, despite Roosevelt's efforts. Even with the fragility of the recovery, the Roosevelt administration decided to raise taxes, slash spending by $1 billion, and reduce the money supply. This produced another devastating recession, with real GDP falling by $5 billion (another example of the multiplier in action). This experience produced an important lesson for economists: When the economy is still in fragile condition from a major recession, it is a mistake to cut spending, raise taxes, or raise interest rates because these can derail the expansion by undermining business and consumer confidence just as they are beginning to rebound. Fortunately, after the financial crisis of 2008–2009, the government heeded that lesson and continued to stimulate the economy until 2017, when the economy had returned to full strength.

World War II proves Keynes right

After 1938, the economy made a sluggish recovery, and it was not until the U.S. entered World War II and engaged in a massive increase in military spending that the Great Depression finally ended. But, World War II did demonstrate conclusively that the government can end any recession, no matter how severe, if it is willing to spend enough money. The wartime spending also proved another of Keynes's ideas true: Running budget deficits for short periods of time does not necessarily create macroeconomic problems. The U.S. government ran huge deficits to finance war spending, but rather than constrain economic development, business investment surged along with government spending. The U.S. public national debt reached 106% of GDP in 1946—the government owed more money than the value of all goods and services produced in a year! Yet, not only did the economy remain strong, but this set the stage for one of the most rapid periods of economic growth that the U.S. has ever seen.

7.5 HAYEK'S CRITIQUE OF GOVERNMENT INTERVENTION

Following the success of Keynesian policy in the U.S. and other countries where it was used, economists became more and more comfortable with the idea of government intervention in the economy to fix market failures. However, one group of economists, the **Austrian** School, led by Ludwig von Mises and Friedrich Hayek, found this approach to be deeply problematic.[4]

The Austrian economists had much in common with neoclassical economic theory, believing that the individual (not groups or institutions) should be the focus of economic analysis. However, they tended to avoid the use of the mathematical models that neoclassical economists favored. Austrian economists also harbored a deep suspicion of government intervention. With the rise of authoritarian regimes on either side of Austria—Nazi Germany and the Soviet Union—this revulsion of government grew even stronger with time.

Hayek was an insightful economist in several key areas, and his ideas had substantial influence on conservative politicians in the U.S. and England. Both Ronald Reagan and Margaret Thatcher cited him as a major influence and inspiration. His often controversial ideas on the business cycle, central planning, freedom, and the efficiency and effectiveness of markets provide an important potential counter-argument to Keynesian approaches.

The business cycle

One of Hayek's major disagreements with Keynes was on the business cycle. Hayek believed that periods of overinvestment create a boom and an imbalance between savings and investment. A shortage of savings causes interest rates to rise, which halts investment and leads to a crash. He thought that, after a crash, financial markets would return to equilibrium, and that there were no major consequences to recessions. In fact, recessions could be useful in his view by weeding out inefficient firms, so recessions should not necessarily be avoided. However, most economists today reject the idea that the government should do nothing to alleviate extraordinarily high levels of bank and business failures and unemployment, believing that the costs of recessions are too high.

Central planning and freedom

Hayek also disagreed with the idea that government should become a welfare state or intervene extensively in industrial development. He saw the New Deal moving the U.S. closer to command communism, and he believed this increased level of government intervention was a threat to freedom, which he defined as freedom from government interference. He argued in *The Road to Serfdom* that "Planning leads to dictatorship because dictatorship is the most effective instrument of coercion and the enforcement of ideals and, as such, essential if central planning on a large scale is to be possible." He worried that any government venture into planning would ultimately lead to dictatorships, so he resisted public health care, public education, and government economic development programs.

In contrast, Karl Polanyi, who wrote *The Great Transformation* during the same time when Hayek was active, thought that Hayek's definition of freedom would result in freedom being available only for the rich and powerful. Polanyi believed that workers and the non-elites needed government intervention to protect them from market outcomes, arguing that unemployment and destitution are "brutal restrictions of freedom." To Polanyi, true freedom, the freedom to live a good life and make choices, comes from having security, a decent income, and job opportunities. He saw government intervention as a crucial part of creating an economy in which everyone, including working people, has significant freedoms.

In Hayek and Polanyi, we see two sides to economic freedom. In philosophy, negative freedom is the absence of barriers or constraints, whereas positive freedom is the ability to have opportunities and to control one's life. Hayek's (negative) definition of freedom emphasizes the right of individuals to do as they will with their person and their property, free from government interference. This view supports a laissez-faire approach in which government plays as little a role as possible. Polanyi's (positive) definition of freedom focuses on the factors that enable most people to live a good life free from the threat of starvation, poverty, and exploitation. This view supports the use of government intervention to regulate the functioning of the economy so that all citizens can live a good life. When we study modern economic systems, we will see this ongoing tension between "freedom from" government, which is the hallmark of most market-dominated (laissez-faire) economies, and "freedom to" have a good life, which is the hallmark of most government-centered economies.

Markets and information

One of Hayek's most important insights was his understanding of markets as superb gatherers and disseminators of information. Hayek pointed out that markets and prices are perfect vehicles for transmitting massive amounts of information to coordinate an economic system. Consumers transmit exactly how much they value goods and how many they want via their purchases. Manufacturers respond to consumer demand by making goods that consumers want in the right quantities. In the process, manufacturers send signals to input markets about what materials they need—how much machinery, raw materials, and labor is required to build their goods. The suppliers of inputs then know how many people they need to hire, and they can figure out what materials they need to obtain for their production. And so on.

One of Hayek's most astute insights was the prediction that the central planning of the Soviet Union could never compete with the efficiency of markets. Planners, he thought, could never duplicate the sophisticated signaling inherent to markets in order to coordinate an entire economy and were doomed to produce inefficiently. Certainly the Soviet Union did run into numerous problems deriving from central planning. Despite developing sophisticated measures of the input requirements for each industry, it regularly experienced gluts or shortages of a huge magnitude that resulted in delays and inefficiencies.

Joseph Schumpeter and creative destruction

In addition to production inefficiencies, the Soviet Union also lagged behind the United States in innovation. A key reason was what another Austrian economist, Joseph Schumpeter, called the "creative destruction" of capitalism. Building on Marx's ideas but coming from a very different perspective, Schumpeter noted that one of the keys to understanding capitalism was the constant innovation and remaking of industries. As he put it in his 1942 book, *Capitalism, Socialism and Democracy*, "The opening up of new markets, foreign or domestic, and the organizational development from the craft shop and factory to such concerns as U.S. Steel illustrate the same process of industrial mutation ... that incessantly revolutionizes the economic structure from within, incessantly destroying the old one, incessantly creating a new one. This process of Creative Destruction is the essential fact about capitalism." *Creative destruction* **is the process by which businesses are forced to invent constantly to stay one step ahead of the competition, and where creative, new industries inevitably destroy and replace older ones.** Certainly capitalism in the U.S. was much more innovative than the command economy of the Soviet Union. While Russia faced a stifling bureaucracy, firms in competitive U.S. capitalist markets were constantly investing and innovating; although, this was less true during the Great Depression than it had been previously.

Schumpeter thought that the process of creative destruction would be too destabilizing for markets, as was the case when entire communities were devastated by the loss of an outmoded industry. Ironically, an adequate safety net can help communities recover from creative destruction and prevent the destabilizing properties of markets from manifesting. So, although Hayek and Schumpeter might not approve given their preference for laissez-faire approaches, modern economies have found a certain amount of government intervention crucial to stabilizing markets, thereby reducing the pressures to rein in markets when communities are suffering from creative destruction, which in turn allows the process of creative destruction to continue.

Market institutions

Hayek also understood that capitalism depends on an important set of supporting institutions in order to function properly. These include the sanctity of private property so that businesses will invest in their enterprises. There also need to be social norms of trust facilitated by systematic and fair laws so that people freely and willingly enter into exchanges and bargains. No one will invest and start a business if they think it will be seized by others once it is successful. Markets also must be contestable—open to the entry of new firms. The government's role, according to Hayek, was to enforce contracts and laws fairly rather than discriminating arbitrarily among individuals. Where market-supporting institutions are absent, markets will not perform effectively, as we see in many cases in less developed countries.

Hayek has had an important influence on economic systems, especially in the U.S. and the U.K. where conservative politicians regularly cite him as a major influence. Even though most economies today utilize more government intervention than Hayek preferred, his cautions about the need to avoid authoritarianism and the inefficiencies of central planning have played a major role in spurring most democracies to impose checks on government behavior.

Next we turn to the U.S. economy in the post-World War II era. We will only cover this period briefly to give you a flavor of the broad sweep of U.S. history and the most important trends.

7.6 THE MIXED ECONOMY AND THE GOLDEN AGE OF U.S. CAPITALISM FROM 1945–1973

The establishment of a mixed economy in the U.S. after the Great Depression and the global dominance of U.S. manufacturing created the perfect combination for a period of unprecedented growth and stability. By the early 1950s, the U.S. was producing 80% of the world's manufacturing output due to its advanced technology and the devastation that other manufacturing industries in Europe and Japan had experienced during World War II.

This era is sometimes termed the "Capital-Labor Accord" in that workers and management got along very well for the most part. Manufacturers could afford to pay their workers well due to their domination of industries, and they had to pay their workers well because unions had become quite powerful now that they were legal. The unionization rate peaked in 1954 with 35% of the work force being represented by a union, and unions were heavily concentrated in manufacturing. Workers experienced rising wages and were able to afford a middle-class lifestyle with a car, a house, and all the appliances and accoutrements that go with a house purchase. The creation of a large middle class in the U.S. stems from this era, and the spending by the middle class proved to be very good for businesses, sparking growth in one consumer industry after another.

The economy grew rapidly and experienced only short recessions in this era, with per capita real GDP growth averaging 2.49% per year from 1948–1973. This was much faster than the per capita real GDP growth rate during the monopoly capitalism era of 1890–1929, when growth averaged 1.92%. It was also faster than growth during the global capitalism era of 1974–2015, which averaged 1.65%. The increase in incomes during the "golden age" was also very equally distributed. Rich, middle-class, and poor citizens all experienced significant increases in income.

Rapid economic growth and strong unions meant that workers received a substantial share of the wealth that was being generated. But firms still benefited significantly as record consumer spending expanded sales and profits. The wealth injected at the bottom to workers trickled up to the owners of businesses.

Despite the rapid growth of the era, African Americans and women were still excluded from the best positions. Overt racial discrimination, separate but unequal education and facilities, and lynchings combined to provoke the Civil Rights movement, led by Martin Luther King. It achieved some major victories, with new laws enacted in the 1960s prohibiting discrimination in employment and preserving voting rights.

Women and minorities were assisted by Affirmative Action laws, which mandated that, in cases where two applicants for a position had equal qualifications but differed by race or gender, the job should go to the person from the under-represented group (women or minorities). This helped pry open jobs in law and business that had previously been the purview of white males.

The government also began intervening more directly in helping the poor. As part of the "War on Poverty," President Lyndon Johnson and Congress established Medicare and Medicaid to provide health care for the poor and the elderly. The Food Stamps program was established, as well as the Head Start program to provide subsidized pre-school for poor children. The government also made its first major attempts to regulate environmental damage. By the end of the 1960s, the government was firmly established in the U.S. as a major factor in markets. However, the stagflation of the 1970s and the deindustrialization associated with globalization that began at the same time would set the stage for a new effort to bring back rapid growth by deregulating the economy.

7.7 THE ERA OF NEOLIBERALISM AND GLOBALIZATION, 1974–2018

In 1973, the Oil Producing and Exporting Countries (OPEC) cut production and imposed an embargo on selling oil to the United States due to U.S. support for Israel. Oil prices surged from $3 per barrel to $12 a barrel internationally (a 300% increase!), and prices were even higher in the U.S. because of the embargo. This devastated the U.S. economy, which had become completely dependent on oil to run its cars and factories. The explosion in the price of energy caused businesses' costs to rise and profits to fall, so they laid off workers. The result was *stagflation*—**stagnation and inflation at the same time**—as businesses laid off workers to cut costs and raised prices to try to recoup the higher cost of energy. A major recession resulted. A second oil crisis occurred in 1979, when oil supplies were disrupted by the Iranian Revolution. This time oil prices doubled, once again spurring a major recession in the U.S. and other oil-dependent economies.

Meanwhile, in a decade that saw two major recessions, there was also a steady erosion of manufacturing jobs due to mechanization and overseas competition from Japan and Europe. Wages for workers stagnated while unemployment and inflation stayed disturbingly high.

Ronald Reagan was elected president in 1980, running on a platform of reducing government and its scope of intervention in the economy—a return to laissez-faire principles. This was known as the era of **neoliberalism**, in that it sought a return to the liberalism of Adam Smith. Many countries followed the lead of Reagan in the U.S. and Thatcher in England, and began moving toward a more laissez-faire economic system.

Reagan was able to enact large tax cuts for businesses and the wealthy, known as supply-side tax cuts because the money went to suppliers (firms and entrepreneurs) rather than demanders (consumers). The Reagan administration also reduced spending on social programs while increasing spending on the military. The U.S. economy did recover by 1984; however, growth in the 1980s was less robust than in previous decades, and the federal deficit quadrupled in size from 1980–1990. The tax cuts did not generate sufficient growth to pay for themselves, as supply-side supporters had hoped. Similar policies emphasizing deregulation and scaling back of government programs were pursued by subsequent presidents George Bush, Bill Clinton, and George W. Bush. Nonetheless, these administrations did follow basic Keynesian stabilization policy, stimulating the economy whenever it hit a recession, so these actions were not a complete reversal of Keynesian policy.

A recession in 1991 was followed by the tech boom of the 1990s under President Clinton. However, a stock market bubble formed towards the end of the 1990s as investors clamored for the latest internet stock offerings, even from companies that had never made a profit. That bubble burst in 2000, with tech stocks plummeting by 78%, and the economy falling into a recession. After a period of modest growth, another bubble formed in the mid-2000s, this time in real estate.

From 2004–2007 a huge speculative bubble, fueled by massive debt and unsound loans in the sub-prime housing market, formed. Deregulation of financial markets pursued by Reagan, Bush, Clinton, and W. Bush allowed banks to invest in very risky and volatile financial instruments. When these investments crashed, they brought the stock market and the entire banking system with them, sparking the worst recession since the Great Depression. Fortunately, the W. Bush administration and, after

2008, the Obama administration, engaged in a massive bailout of the banking system and a significant increase in government spending. Rather than repeat the errors of 1937 and the Great Depression, the Fed kept stimulating the economy by injecting money into financial markets for years after the worst part of the recession was over. Obama also signed the Affordable Care Act, making the U.S. the last developed country to install a national health care system of some kind. Keynesian policy had returned to the U.S., and it reduced the length of the recession significantly. As conclusive evidence of how useful Keynesian policy is, the European Union, which imposed austerity programs on the economies of Greece, Spain, and other poorly performing economies, fared very poorly compared to the U.S., which instead injected large amounts of money into the economy.

The recovery from the Great Recession was slow, as is often the case after a major financial crisis. Hoping for a change in policies that would reinvigorate economic growth, U.S. voters elected Donald Trump president in 2016. Trump promised to bring back jobs to the U.S. from abroad by renegotiating trade deals and by cutting taxes and regulations on businesses. In essence, Trump was promising more government intervention in some areas (trade) and less in others (deregulation). The unrest that propelled Trump to the presidency was also present in other developed economies where workers' wages stagnated and communities experienced deindustrialization as jobs shifted to China and other inexpensive manufacturing locations. Whether this will lead to a significant move away from neoliberalism remains to be seen.

7.8 CONCLUSION: THE MIXED ECONOMY OF THE U.S.

In general, there has been a trend toward greater deregulation in the U.S. since 1980, but the country continues to use government policy and programs to fix market failures. The U.S. is a laissez-faire-leaning mixed economy, with less government intervention than most other developed countries but much more government intervention than was the case in the U.S. prior to the Great Depression. Keynesian economic policy has been very good for the U.S. economy in general. As you can see from Figure 7.2, prior to 1950, the U.S. economy experienced dramatic fluctuations in economic growth. After 1950, the U.S. experienced more rapid and steady growth, which was achieved with the help of government efforts to stabilize the economy. A stable business environment makes firms more likely to invest, which drives growth and prosperity.

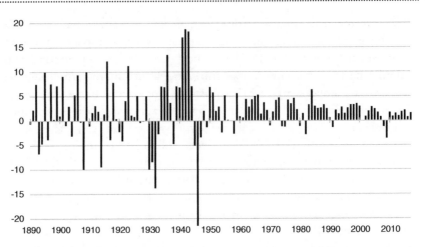

FIGURE 7.3 Economic instability in the U.S. economy: Real GDP growth per capita, 1890–2017.

Source: Our World in Data, https://ourworldindata.org/grapher/gdp-per-capita-over-the-long-run-Maddison, World Bank and St. Louis Fed (FRED).

This type of economic system is called "regulated capitalism" or a *mixed economy*: **Where markets are seen as worth preserving due to the efficiency and innovation they promote, but sound government policy can improve the functioning of the capitalist market system by reducing or eliminating market failures such as recessions.** A mixed economy relying on markets and government is seen by most economists as preferable to a laissez-faire or a state-dominated economy.

Keynes can be thought of as wanting to save capitalism from itself. In its unregulated state, capitalism can result in lengthy recessions, as well as bad outcomes for workers and the environment. Appropriate government policy can solve those problems. In a recession, the government can spend money, cut taxes, and increase the money supply to pump money back into the economy and, via the multiplier, increase spending significantly to end the recession. If banks are prone to speculative bubbles and risky behavior, the government can regulate them to make sure they behave in a financially sound manner. Where markets fail to safeguard workers or the environment, the government can impose laws or regulations to force markets to address these shortcomings.

As we will see in the next chapter, which looks at modern economic systems, other economies strive for a different balance of state and markets than the U.S. The U.S. is a **market dominated economy**, striving for the least amount of government intervention possible to keep markets functioning effectively. Even though our government is large, it controls only about 30% of the economy while the rest of the economy is controlled by private sector firms. In other countries, such as most of Europe and Japan, we find **social market economies** where the government controls a much larger share (sometimes over 50%) and strives to manage the economy in accordance with domestic social values. Meanwhile, in **state-dominated economies** like China, the government plays an even larger role in controlling the economic system. All of these economic systems use some degree of markets and some amount of government intervention, so they are all considered mixed market economies, but the mix of market and government can be quite different.

• •

QUESTIONS FOR REVIEW

1. Explain how the neoclassical concepts (a) Marginal Productivity Theory of Distribution, (b) Markets Always Clear, and (c) Say's Law combine to result in a conclusion that no government intervention is necessary in a capitalist market system.
2. Describe the nature of the Keynesian "revolution" in economics. How did Keynes reshape the way economists thought about the economy? How did he address the major flaws in the neoclassical economics of his time?
3. Why do many economists see the volatility of investment along with the multiplier as the key to understanding the business cycle (the cycle of booms and busts that characterize our economic system)?
4. How do sticky wages and prices prevent the economy from adjusting in a recession?
5. In what areas of the economy do we tend to see the market fail to work well? What government programs have been designed to address those market failures?
6. How would you explain to someone with no economics background why deflation can be a major macroeconomic problem?
7. How do Keynes' ideas relate to those of Smith and Marx?
8. Which of Keynes' ideas do you find most compelling in capturing the realities of the modern world? Explain and give examples.
9. Which of Hayek's ideas do you find most compelling? Which are least compelling? Support your answer with examples and analysis.
10. Compare and contrast Keynes' ideas with those of Hayek.
11. Explain the concept of creative destruction, and give examples from the world around us.
12. Describe the evolution of the U.S. economic system from 1920 to the present. How has our approach to regulating the economy shifted over time?

NOTES

1. Cannan, Edwin, "The Demand for Labour," *The Economic Journal*, September 1932, pp. 357–370 (pages 367, 369).

2. Source: https://commons.wikimedia.org/wiki/File:Lord_Keynes.jpg.

3. Wolman, Leo, "Wages During the Depression," National Bureau of Economic Research Bulletin, Number 46, May 1, 1933, pp. 1–5. www.nber.org/chapters/c2256.pdf

4. The founder of the Austrian school is considered to be Carl Menger, who taught at the University of Vienna in Austria in the late 1800s. Although later scholars from this tradition worked and lived outside of Austria, the original label stuck.

Modern economic systems

Market Dominated, Social Market, and State Dominated Economies

The economic systems of the modern world draw extensively on the ideas and philosophies of the great economists. From Smith, we see the widespread use of markets and the tendency to allow firms to compete and to make major economic decisions for society based on the profit motive. From Marx and Veblen, we see the need to check the unfettered power of large firms and to safeguard workers and communities from exploitation. From Hayek and Smith, we see the need to check the coercive power of the state to prevent it from becoming too powerful and bureaucratic. From Keynes, we see the approach that dominates modern economic systems: The construction of a mixed economy which builds on the best aspects of market capitalism while regulating market failures is likely to deliver the best outcomes.

All modern economies combine a mix of markets and government to some degree. Even Market Dominated Economies, such as the U.S. economy, have a substantial amount of government (state) intervention. And even State Dominated Economies, such as China, Cuba, and North Korea, use markets, often extensively. The key to understanding modern economic systems is therefore to grasp the mix of state and market in a particular economy.

In general, we can group economies into 3 broad categories.

1. Market Dominated Economies (MDEs), also called liberal market economies, are economic systems in which the primary economic decisions are made by private actors (businesses, individuals) in the market. Government and social values play a secondary role.

2. Social Market Economies (SMEs), also called coordinated market economies, are economic systems in which social values take a leading role in directing the economy, usually through the actions of a government which manages the economy in accordance with social values.

3. State Dominated Economies (SDEs) are economic systems in which the government is the main economic actor in most major industries or economic decisions, owning or controlling most of the economy.

This chapter will briefly survey the different types of successfully developed economic systems in the world and offer some case studies of each type. (We consider developing countries here.) We begin by contrasting MDEs and SMEs, followed by a case study of the U.S. MDE and the Nordic SME. Next, we take up socialism and communism, which culminates in a case study of China's SDE.

8.0 CHAPTER 8 LEARNING GOALS

After reading this chapter you should be able to:

- Define and describe the characteristics of Market Dominated Economies, Social Market Economies, and State Dominated Economies;
- Analyze, compare, and contrast the characteristics and functioning of an MDE such as the United States, an SME such as the Nordic countries, and an SDE such as China;
- Explain the difference between socialism, communism, and capitalism; and,
- Evaluate the strengths and weaknesses of a market capitalist approach (U.S.), a guided market approach (Nordic Model), and a central planning approach (USSR) to economic development.

8.1 COMPARING MARKET DOMINATED ECONOMIES AND SOCIAL MARKET ECONOMIES

Most of the world's developed economies are either Market Dominated Economics or Social Market Economies. We begin by describing and comparing those economies and looking at their effectiveness as economic systems in delivering economic growth and human well-being.

In Market Dominated Economies, most major economic decisions are made by corporations and other private sector businesses. These businesses determine what society produces and how it is produced. The private sector dictates how a society's scarce resources are allocated based on the profit motive and businesses' desire to persuade consumers to buy more of their products.

The government's major role in MDEs is to support the market system by building and maintaining infrastructure (roads, airports, ports, a postal system), providing a fair and effective judicial system that enforces contracts, and fixing market failures when they threaten the functioning of the market system. The major market failures that are usually addressed by government include macroeconomic instability (especially major recessions), poverty and inequality, the exploitation of laborers and the environment, and the lack of sufficient private health or education.

Interestingly, when we look at wealthy countries in the world that have adopted a market dominated economic system (the United States, Canada, Ireland, Australia, New Zealand, and the United Kingdom), we see that they were all part of the British Empire at one point. The culture and values of that empire, emphasizing Protestantism, self-interest, hard work, and material rewards, fits well with a market economy. In this sense, MDEs reflect a particular set of cultural values.

In Social Market Economies, the role of social interests is more balanced compared to the role of the market. Social values often take precedence over market outcomes in SMEs. Some economic decisions are made by markets, especially those related to consumer goods. Many, and sometimes most, decisions are made by society, acting through government. Many services are considered to be human rights, including health care, child care, dental care, housing, education (including college), and even a job. The government is charged with providing all citizens with these services, sometimes through government agencies and sometimes by working with and through the private sector. In SMEs, the state can also play a role in preserving domestic culture, such as the French government's efforts to protect traditional agriculture, food, and wine.

Although the SMEs represent a variety of very different cultures, they do have some commonalities. While England was the first country to industrialize, countries that industrialized later usually utilized government intervention to spur industrialization and to catch up with England. SMEs, therefore, are accustomed to a larger degree of government intervention in determining the direction of the economy. Most SMEs have industrial policies which they use to stimulate economic development in key sectors in order to gain advantages in these industries relative to other countries.

Lest you be tempted to think that one of these models is superior to the other, consider carefully the data in Figure 8.1, which compares key economic indicators of the largest and wealthiest MDEs and SMEs in the world.

Market Dominated Economies	GDP devoted to social expenditures, 2013	Tax Revenue as a % of GDP, 2015	Real GDP per capita, 2016	Growth in Real GDP per capita, 1971-2016	Poverty Rate, 2013
Canada	16.9%	31.2%	$ 42,392	74.5%	12.6%
Australia	18.1%	27.8%	$ 45,083	75.5%	12.8%
United States	18.8%	25.9%	$ 52,066	82.0%	17.5%
New Zealand	19.3%	32.5%	$ 34,211	62.2%	10.9%
United Kingdom	21.9%	32.1%	$ 38,460	86.4%	10.5%
MDE Average	**19.0%**	**29.9%**	**$ 42,442**	**76.1%**	**12.9%**

Social Market Economies					
Norway	21.8%	38.7%	$ 59,366	104.3%	8.1%
Netherlands	22.9%	37.5%	$ 46,125	78.8%	7.7%
Japan	23.1%	32.0%	$ 37,492	96.9%	16.0%
Germany	24.8%	36.6%	$ 42,894	85.4%	9.5%
Sweden	27.4%	42.8%	$ 45,030	77.1%	9.0%
Denmark	29.0%	49.6%	$ 44,752	69.6%	5.5%
Belgium	29.3%	45.0%	$ 41,249	82.9%	9.1%
France	31.5%	45.5%	$ 37,272	75.0%	8.2%
SME Average	**26.2%**	**41.0%**	**$ 44,274**	**83.8%**	**9.1%**

FIGURE 8.1 Key data on selected MDEs and SMEs.

Source: OECD, http://stats.oecd.org, 2017.

First, a good indicator of whether or not a country is an MDE or an SME is the amount of its GDP devoted by the public sector to social expenditures, such as health, welfare, unemployment, job assistance, and child care. Social expenditures also go along with a high tax rate: If you spend a lot on social services for your citizens then you have to raise a lot of tax revenue. As you can see from the first two columns of Figure 8.1, MDEs tend to spend less on social expenditures and have lower taxes than SMEs.

One of the key issues for economists when evaluating an economic system is how well it performs. column 3 displays Real GDP per capita in MDEs and SMEs, while column 4 looks at the rate of growth in GDP per capita over the last 45 years. Interestingly, there is no clear pattern. Both MDEs and SMEs are rich, and both have experienced substantial economic growth (1.69% per year in MDEs, 1.86% per year in SMEs). There is no reason to prefer one system over another based on growth performance: An effective MDE can perform just as well as an effective SME. Where we do see significant differences are in terms of inequality. Because of the substantial amount of money devoted to social expenditures, SMEs tend to have very low levels of poverty and inequality. MDEs that spend less on these programs have much higher levels of poverty and inequality.

Another way to look at the success of economic systems is to consider a broad range of indicators. For example, the OECD Better Life Index ranks OECD countries according to the following factors: Housing,

Country (MDE or SME)	OECD Better Life Index Ranking, 2016	UN Human Development Index Ranking, 2016
Norway (SME)	1	1
Australia (MDE)	2	2
Denmark (SME)	3	5
Switzerland (SME)	4	2
Canada(MDE)	5	10
Sweden (SME)	6	14
New Zealand (MDE)	7	13
Finland (SME)	8	23
United States (MDE)	9	10
Iceland (SME)	10	9
Netherlands (SME)	11	7
Germany (SME)	12	4
Belgium (SME)	13	22
Austria (SME)	14	24
United Kingdom (MDE)	15	16
Ireland (MDE)	16	8
France (SME)	17	21
Spain (SME)	18	27
Japan (SME)	22	17
Italy (SME)	24	26

FIGURE 8.2 OECD Better Life and UN Human Development Rankings, 2016.

income, jobs, community, education, environment, civic engagement, health, life satisfaction, safety, and work-life balance. The United Nations (UN) Human Development Index focuses on a subset of the OECD measures: Life expectancy, education, and income per capita indicators. Notice that the Scandinavian countries (Norway, Denmark, Sweden, Finland, and Iceland) do particularly well on these broader measures of welfare, something we will discuss below when we take up the Nordic Model. Nonetheless, both MDEs and SMEs perform well for the most part, providing another indication that there are different paths to wealth and well-being.

Next, we take up case studies of each type of economic system. We begin by describing the unique characteristics of the modern U.S. MDE relative to other economics systems. We follow that with a case study of the Nordic Model of SMEs. Then we take up State Dominated Economies, focusing primarily on China.

8.2 THE UNITED STATES MODEL OF A MARKET DOMINATED ECONOMY

Having traced the evolution of the U.S. economy in previous chapters, here we only describe the key aspects of the U.S. system as they compare to other economies. The major characteristics of the U.S. economic system include ready access to productive resources, a Protestant work ethic and melting pot of immigrants, early protectionism followed by later globalization, a business-friendly legal system, massive multinational corporations, an innovation system promoting revolutionary innovations, a small welfare state and few regulations, and macroeconomic stabilization policies.

Ready access to productive resources

One of the important reasons for U.S. economic success was its access to human and natural resources. The U.S. has historically had a large pool of mobile and highly motivated immigrant labor. Immigrant groups included religious dissidents, people pursuing commercial enterprises, convicts, indentured servants, slaves, and waves of migrants from Europe. The U.S. also had rich land and abundant natural resources, acquired via war, negotiation or purchase, which were crucial in agricultural and industrial development. This ready supply of labor and resources provided fuel for economic growth.

Protestant work ethic and the melting pot

The U.S. has a culture that is very hard working and individualistic. This is often attributed to that fact that many of the early settlers were Protestants who valued personal independence and material success. Later immigrants from Europe, Mexico, India, China, and many other countries also tended to be extremely hard working and willing to take the least desirable jobs just so that they or their children would have a chance to move up in the future. Hard work is so ingrained into the U.S. culture that American workers put in more hours than most other developed countries, and surveys indicate that social status is strongly associated with hard work. Highly motivated labor facilitates production and growth.

Early protectionism, later globalization

The split with Great Britain in the Revolutionary War prompted the U.S. to protect its market from British competitors, which allowed domestic industries to develop and sell to the large, internal U.S. market.

This allowed infant industries that would not have been able to survive otherwise to grow and develop. However, after World War II, the U.S. increasingly embraced globalization and free trade now that its industries dominated international manufacturing. U.S. corporations moved their operations all over the globe in search of new markets and cheap labor and resources.

Business friendly legal system

The stable U.S. constitution and a pro-business legal system provided solid grounding for market exchange. Checks and balances with an independent judiciary tended to keep corruption to an acceptable level and to safeguard contracts and property rights. Civil liberties and democratic rule meant that many citizens had opportunities to succeed and to change the system; although, this was mitigated by systemic racism and sexism. Corporations were given substantial power in the U.S. system, including legal standing as a person with all the rights that citizens have, along with low taxes and other forms of government support. As we saw earlier, the U.S. government sided with corporations and against workers throughout much of its history.

Massive multinational corporations

U.S. corporations were allowed to grow into vast, market-dominating enterprises that controlled entire global industries. The typical U.S. Multinational Corporation (MNC) is huge and very hierarchical, with power and decision-making resting in the hands of the Chief Executive Officer (CEO) and upper administration. Workers tend to have very little power and control, given the low unionization rates in the modern U.S. and in the countries in which MNCs operate. These huge companies are almost all owned by shareholders, and their shares are traded publicly in stock markets, so their primary goal is to maximize short-term profits to please shareholders. Massive MNCs dominate the U.S. and much of the world economy.

Innovation system promoting revolutionary innovation

The U.S. government has always invested substantially in public goods, especially infrastructure, building canals, railroads, roads, ports, and airports to stimulate economic development. Free public education and the vast public university system helped to develop a skilled work force and to stimulate scientific research, which fostered numerous inventions. A 2017 study published in *Science* found that 80 percent of high-impact scientific papers (those cited frequently by other scientists) can be traced forward to some future marketplace invention, demonstrating how crucial basic scientific research is for innovation.[1] The strong patent system in the U.S., which gives inventors a monopoly over their new product for 20 years, also provides a strong incentive for investment and innovation. The combination of low taxes on corporations and wealthy individuals, along with strong higher education and patent systems, and a hard-working, individualistic culture provides excellent conditions to prompt people to come up with the next big product. The U.S. is one of the world leaders in revolutionary innovation (inventing brand-new products and industries) due to these conditions.

Small welfare state and few regulations

In general, the U.S. has the least generous welfare state of any developed country. The most glaring difference is in the area of health care: The U.S. is the only developed country without a national health care system. Even other MDEs consider basic health care a human right that should not be left up to the market to provide, meaning that millions who cannot afford health care will have to do without it, or to depend on charity. The Affordable Care Act (ACA) enacted by President Obama caused the number of uninsured in the U.S. to decline from a high of 18% in 2013, just before the Affordable Care Act went into effect, to 11% in 2017. However, there remain political pressures to repeal or replace the ACA from conservative politicians who preferred to leave health care in the hands of individuals and markets.

The U.S. also does less to address inequality and poverty than any other developed country. Taxes on the wealthy are relatively low, while financial assistance for the poor for housing, food, child care, dental care, and higher education is also low. Welfare and unemployment benefits are also less generous, and the U.S. provides very little in the way of job training. This explains why the U.S. has the highest poverty rate of any developed country.

The U.S. tends to have fewer regulations on business behavior than other countries, with relatively lax approaches to regulating the environment, labor markets, and food and product safety. The U.S. has the highest per-person carbon emissions in the world, but it has yet to take significant steps to address climate change, unlike most other developed countries.

Note that we are discussing the U.S. in comparison to other countries. Despite the tendency to have fewer regulations than other countries, the U.S. still regulates food and drug safety, water and air quality, traffic safety, agricultural safety, workplace safety, and consumer product safety.

Macroeconomic stabilization policy

While the U.S. does not intervene much in specific (microeconomic) markets, it does take an activist role in stabilizing the macroeconomy to reduce the severity of recessions and to stave off inflation. The U.S. government spends more, taxes less, and injects more money into financial markets in most recessions. This is very distinct from the European Union (EU), which adopted austerity policies that slashed spending and raised taxes while keeping interest rates stable after the 2008 financial crisis. Ironically, while the EU intervenes less in the macroeconomy, most corporations and markets in the EU are tightly regulated, with strict laws regarding environment, workers, and product safety.

In general, the U.S. is the quintessential model of a market dominated, mixed economy. Most decisions are made by private sector firms and individuals while the government corrects the most egregious forms of market failure but does not take more proactive steps. The model has worked well in terms of generating economic growth and a steady stream of innovations. Those successes are marred somewhat by the inequality, poverty, and environmental degradation that are generated in the process. Interestingly, the Nordic countries are also wealthy and innovative, but their success is achieved in a more government-centered economic system.

8.3 THE NORDIC MODEL OF A SOCIAL MARKET ECONOMY

The Nordic Model is often referred to as the "middle way" between the two extremes of a Market Dominated Economy and a State Dominated Economy. The Nordic countries—Sweden, Norway, Denmark, Iceland, and Finland—are considered SMEs because of the manner in which their egalitarian social values inform government intervention in their economies. They are ultimately still capitalist economies utilizing markets for many economic decisions, but their governments play a much larger role than is the case in MDEs. One of the interesting questions for economists is why this region of the world evolved more cooperative, egalitarian systems than most other regions.

Cooperative culture and homogeneous population

Driven by the harsh climate of northern Europe, Scandinavians were forced to work hard and to cooperate in order to survive. The cooperative culture has persisted into the modern era in part due to its success—all the Nordic countries are wealthy. In addition, the homogeneity and small size of the population tends to foster empathy. When someone in a Nordic country is destitute, it is easy for their neighbors to imagine that they too might experience the same fate. Note, however, that the Nordic countries were not particularly equal 100 years ago. It took powerful, well-organized labor movements to create the Nordic model over the last century. This, of course, implies that any country in which workers have strong solidarity and organization might be able to emulate the Nordic model.

Gender equity

Another area in which we see the Nordic culture at work in affecting market outcomes is gender equity. A Norwegian law requires 40% of corporate boards of directors to be women so that it is more likely that larger numbers of women will be selected for upper management. Norway's parental leave policies are quite generous, as are those of other Nordic countries. Together, Norwegian parents are allowed to take 46 weeks off at 100% of pay, or 56 weeks off at 80% of pay. Employers are required to allow workers to return to their old jobs at the end of parental leave, which means that there is little or no detriment to your career if you choose to have children. The employment guarantee, along with free child care, result in 75% of Norwegian women working outside the home, as opposed to 68% in the U.S. There are also payments for parents who choose to be stay-at-home parents.

With similarly generous policies, in 2015, the 5 Nordic countries ranked at the very top of the world in terms of best places to be a mother, while the U.S. ranked 33rd. The U.S. only requires employers to grant new mothers 4 weeks of unpaid maternity leave. The intentional efforts by Nordic countries to create greater gender equity have spilled over into the political realm. 40% of representatives in Parliament in Nordic countries are women, compared with 19.4% in the U.S.

Dramatic expansion of human rights

The egalitarian culture led Nordic countries to expand the definition of human rights well beyond what we find in MDEs. All Nordic citizens have the right to child care, health care, dental care, free education (through college), housing, and food. These essentials are either provided by government agencies, or the government subsidizes the private sector to provide them. The government invests substantially in all of these services so that they are of very high quality. As one might expect, the provision of such extensive services comes with a hefty price tag, which requires high tax rates in order to pay for them.

Government-guided development

Rather than letting market forces determine the direction of the economy, the state in Nordic countries guides and facilitates economic development with a sophisticated set of policies. Sweden, for example, is famous for its "triple helix" economic development approach utilizing government, universities, and the private sector. In the 1970s and 1980s, Sweden began experiencing deindustrialization in the face of increased global competition, just as the U.S. did. Rather than trying to save dying industries, Sweden implemented an initiative to attract new high wage industries based on government, university, and private sector partnerships. The government would identify new, key industries that were likely to generate high wage jobs and that were suitable for the local economy. These industries included biotechnology, research and development, computer programming, and information technology. After consulting with private sector firms, the government would provide state-of-the-art infrastructure, and universities would provide training and education to make sure that the work force had exactly the right set of skills. This made Sweden an ideal location for industries in the targeted sectors, attracting a huge influx of foreign investment, and leading to the creation of new jobs in each of the above industries. This focus on cutting-edge industries, education, and research and development has resulted in Sweden generating more patent filings per resident than the U.S.

Note that other countries, including Japan and South Korea, have also been very successful in targeting cutting-edge industries and developing them via substantial state support. Many economists see such industrial policies as a key step in developing an industrial sector in an underdeveloped region. However, such policies require an efficient, non-corrupt government sector. In countries with poor quality state institutions, industrial policies have not worked well.

Another interesting example of state-guided development is Norway's state oil company, Statoil. This public company was created to manage North Sea oil drilling to ensure that all Norwegian citizens benefitted from the oil discoveries. The government places all profits from Statoil into an Oil Fund which is used to pay for much of the Norwegian welfare state and to provide Norway with economic security in the future, even after the oil runs out. The government treats the Oil Fund like an endowment, spending only the interest and 4% of the principal in any year. In 2017, the Oil Fund was valued at $958 billion, which was almost 1% of global equity markets!

We also see substantial government intervention in Sweden's ultra-Keynesian macroeconomic policies. Sweden was the first country to use Keynesian stabilization policies extensively, beginning in the early years of the Great Depression. In addition to generous unemployment and welfare benefits, Sweden provides public employment for many of those who cannot find jobs otherwise. The idea is that in each community there are plenty of tasks that need to be done. The government should hire those willing and able to work but unable to find a private sector job to complete useful tasks, in the process pumping money into the economy. Businesses are also allowed to make tax free investments if they do so in a recession, which stimulates investment when it is needed most. Sweden recovered very rapidly from the 2008 financial crisis thanks to these stabilization policies.

Active labor market policies (flexicurity)

When workers in Sweden lose their job, they are given generous benefits with a time limit, and provided with free education, training, and money for relocation costs so that they can find a new job. If they are still unable to find a job at that point, they can get a job on a public works project. This makes Sweden's labor market flexible in that workers are regularly moving from one job to another, but it also offers workers significant job security because they will almost always have a job or state support. Note that this is not a "soft" system—everyone is expected to work. These flexicurity programs resulted in Sweden having the highest rate of labor market participation in the world (the highest percentage of the population working).

It is also interesting that, like the U.S., Nordic countries are hotbeds for entrepreneurship and innovation. Startup rates in Norway are among the highest in the developed world, and Norway has more entrepreneurs per capita than the U.S. This can be traced to state support for entrepreneurs in Norway. First, the security of the welfare state means that you have little to lose if your business fails. If it does fail, you will still get guaranteed retirement and health benefits, along with education and training for a new job. Free college education means that you have no student loan debt that has to be paid off if your business fails, so you can start a business right out of college. There are free courses on starting a business, you can get a state-sponsored 3-month internship in a start-up company, and it is easy to start a company, taking only 7 days.

Inequality and poverty

As Figure 8.1 shows, the poverty rate in the Nordic countries is half that of the U.S. This reflects the disparate levels of government spending to fight poverty and create opportunities for the poor. Similarly, the U.S. is the most unequal developed country while the Nordic countries are the most equal in terms of income and wealth, which is reflected in the differences in tax policies. Sweden imposes a 1.5% annual wealth tax on rich individuals whereas the U.S. has no wealth tax, and the richest people in Sweden pay 60% of their income in taxes whereas the tax rate for the richest Americans is 39.6%. The 400 richest families in the U.S. only paid 20% of their income in taxes thanks to a plethora of tax deductions and low taxes on investment income.

Greater equality is also associated with a greater likelihood of moving up in the world. There is significantly greater class mobility in Nordic countries than in the U.S. Statistically, a poor child in Denmark has a 22% chance of becoming rich, while a poor child in the United States has only a 1% chance. This disparity is a product of the greater resources available to poor children in Denmark, especially high quality education and health care, which give them a better chance to succeed.

In general, we see in the Nordic Model a set of countries that is globally competitive because of their effective use of the state to facilitate economic development. They also have exceptionally high measures of human development because of their use of heavily progressive taxes to provide high quality services and support for all citizens.

8.4 OTHER VARIETIES OF SOCIAL MARKET ECONOMIES

Because there is so much variety in Social Market Economies, it is worthwhile documenting some of the ways in which other SMEs differ from the Nordic Model and reflect unique sets of cultural and institutional factors. Below, we briefly describe some of the unique characteristics of the largest SMEs, Germany, France, and Japan.

Germany, co-determination and precision manufacturing

Germany is a world leader in producing high value manufactured goods such as robotics, cars, and electronics. The German emphasis on technology is reflected in the fact that most CEOs of manufacturing firms are engineers, whereas in the U.S. it is more common to find CEOs with finance or marketing backgrounds. German education has two tracks, one targeting college and the other the development of sophisticated vocational skills that will culminate in an internship and a skilled job. Workers in Germany are extremely well paid, as you can see in Figure 8.3, whereas U.S. workers make $10 less per hour. German workers also have substantial input into how work is done, and at large firms workers elect members to the supervisory boards of corporations that

Country	Hourly Compensation ($)
Norway	63.36
Switzerland	57.79
Belgium	52.19
Sweden	49.80
Denmark	48.47
Australia	47.68
Germany	45.79
Finland	42.60
Austria	41.53
France	39.81
Netherlands	39.62
Ireland	38.17
Canada	36.59
United States	35.67
Japan	35.34
Italy	34.18
United Kingdom	31.23
Spain	26.83
New Zealand	24.77
Singapore	24.16
Korea, Republic of	20.72

FIGURE 8.3 Hourly compensation costs in manufacturing, 2012.

Source: www.bls.gov/fls/#compensation.

appoint the members of the board of directors. This system is called co-determination because both workers and firms together make major decisions regarding the future of the company.[2] Thus, German workers have much more input into how corporations are run than American workers do. This has translated into an empowered work force that displays some of the highest productivity and greatest skill levels in the world. Interestingly, while Germany is a highly regulated economy, it tends to avoid substantial macroeconomic intervention, a philosophy which it has carried over into the EU.

France, fashion, and leisure

France is another large, wealthy country in which cultural considerations play a large role in structuring the economy. The French work very hard to preserve their culture and way of life. This includes strict rules designed to preserve local food sources and cuisine. Correspondingly, France has very strong culturally-based industries, including tourism (France is the most visited destination in the world) and fashion. France is home to the world's two largest luxury products companies, LVMH (Moët Hennessy Louis Vuitton) and Kering (Gucci, Yves San Laurent, etc.).

The French government also works as a member of the European Union to guide and protect established industries such as clothing and steel. It is well-known for utilizing expert government planners to work with industry to construct economic development programs. In addition to guiding the economy, the government imposes strict regulations on businesses, including laws that make it difficult for firms to fire workers or to close an unprofitable manufacturing plant.

After it experienced the same forces of deindustrialization that hit other developed countries, France decided to deal with its high unemployment rate by reducing work hours for existing laborers and increasing leisure time. The maximum work week was reduced to 35 hours, or 39 hours for CEOs and upper management. (This did reduce the unemployment rate, although France still has chronically high unemployment.) To enforce the law, the government hired inspectors to count cars in parking lots after business hours, scrutinize office entry and computer records, grill employees about their schedules, and make sure no one was bringing work home with them! (Isn't there something appealing about a government inspector telling you to go home because you are working too hard?)

With the short work week, 5 weeks of paid vacation and 11 paid holidays, the French work fewer hours than most other countries. France and the U.S. both generate about $60 in GDP per hour worked, so the main reason GDP per capita in the U.S. is higher than France is because people in the U.S. work 19% more hours than the French do. Essentially, the French work 4 days a week while Americans work 5 days a week, on average. This brings up an interesting question: Would you rather have more money or more leisure time? The French have chosen the latter.

Japan, keiretsu, and lifetime employment

Japan has the 3rd-largest economy in the world, behind the U.S. and China and just ahead of Germany, the United Kingdom, and France. As with other SMEs, Japan's unique culture shapes its economy in significant ways. Like France, Japan's government uses highly skilled planners to work with industry to determine the direction of the economy. Top university graduates often go into government work and then move from government to industry leadership positions, which is a sign of how highly valued public service is.

As a deeply Confucian society featuring an emphasis on respect for elders, loyalty, and harmony, Japan has evolved unique organizational structures. The Japanese economy is dominated by 6 huge conglomerates, known as keiretsu. Each keiretsu is owned primarily by a bank, and these banks tend to prefer long term growth and steady returns over short term profits. This gives Japanese corporations a much longer focus than we tend to see in U.S. corporations. Within each keiretsu one finds networks of companies working together for a common goal. For example, Toyota works closely with all of its suppliers so that production changes can be made swiftly and seamlessly with minimal disruptions. This close integration of Toyota with all of its suppliers within the same keiretsu reduces costs, fosters innovation, and allows Toyota to respond more rapidly to changes in consumer preferences.

Within each large corporation, employees tend to act like an extended family. It is common for employees at the top Japanese firms to stay at the same firm for their entire career—lifetime employment! Workers socialize together, and promotions often come from within the company. This family-like atmosphere fosters cooperation and loyalty, leading to high levels of productivity and trust and a flat organizational structure in which workers need little supervision.

In all of the SMEs we see much larger government involvement in the strategic direction of the economy, with government planners working with industry officials to determine what industries to focus on and where to invest. Government regulation of the economy is more in line with local social values than it is with the market. Some commentators call such economies "socialist", but private sector firms still dominate most industries, so SMEs are actually still mixed market capitalist systems. True socialism or communism is a very different system, as we will discuss in the next section.

8.5 SOCIALISM AND COMMUNISM

Anyone who has experienced the dark side of capitalism—especially poorly paid workers abused by powerful, uncaring bosses—has likely longed for an alternative economic system. Since the very beginnings of capitalism more than 200 years ago, the downtrodden have turned to socialism and communism as a possible solution to the problems with capitalism.

A socialist economic system is one in which the means of production and distribution are either owned or regulated by society. Note that in most SMEs, only 40-60% of the economy is controlled or regulated by the state, whereas a fully socialist system would mean control or regulation of almost all industries. A communist economic system is one in which the means of production and distribution are publicly owned and each person works according to their abilities and is paid according to their needs. Socialism can be considered the first step of an economy on the way toward communism. In general, communist systems involve central planning, with the government determining what is produced, how it is produced, who does what job, and how goods and services are distributed. State ownership and control of the economy is nearly absolute.

Beginning with the Russian Revolution of 1917, numerous countries experienced communist uprisings in the 20th century. Just before the fall of the Union of Soviet Socialist Republics (USSR) in Russia in 1989, a third of the world's population lived in a communist country. However, although Marx proposed communism as a solution to the problems of capitalism, he never laid out how a communist system would work in practice. Countries attempting to implement communism had no blueprint to follow, so they had no choice but to try various methods and hope that they worked.

The USSR developed a system of central planning where the state made all major economic decisions. Fearing invasion by the United States and other hostile capitalist countries, the USSR undertook an effort to industrialize a previously rural and backward economic system. Planners instructed every industry on what to produce, along with when and how to produce it. They set up elaborate input-output tables for the entire economy detailing every input needed for every product so that they could allocate the correct resources in the right quantities to each manufacturer. They focused on manufacturing and especially on defense, given the external threats they faced.

Initially, this system was remarkably successful. While most of the world was experiencing the Great Depression, the economy of the USSR grew rapidly, between 4 and 13 percent per year. The Soviet Union succeeded in industrializing a previously rural, agrarian economy with remarkable speed. This success prompted worries in western capitalist countries, where it appeared that the communist system was more successful than capitalism.

But it was not to last. The centralization of control allowed ruthless dictators like Joseph Stalin to seize power in the USSR. Stalin killed more than a million people during his time as Soviet General Secretary and Premier. As the bureaucracy became more entrenched, efficiency declined, and the USSR began to experience regular shortages of inputs and even basic consumer goods.

Most other communist countries who imitated the Soviet central planning model experienced similar problems. In places where control was more decentralized, however, more positive results were achieved. And, in places in which local culture was already communal in nature, the system worked reasonably well.

In Cuba, while political power was controlled by the communist party under Fidel Castro, workers had substantial power and control over the workplace. This is an ironic reversal of the U.S., where workers have the political power that comes with voting but lack power in the workplace. Cuba was able to achieve impressive results in education, literacy, and health, reaching levels of developed countries. Cuba's economic growth averaged 2% from 1990–2016, which is impressive given that it faced a huge cut in subsidies when the USSR collapsed in 1990 and that it has continually faced U.S. economic sanctions during that period.

Yugoslavia, like Cuba, gave workers substantial control over workplaces, developing a series of worker-owned cooperatives as the basic organizational unit. They experienced some substantial successes before being derailed by regional and ethnic differences.

After a century of efforts by various countries to construct communist economic systems, the following lessons have emerged:

- Central planning can be a good way to organize and mobilize resources to industrialize in societies that were previously underdeveloped;
- Central planning does not tend to be as dynamic, efficient, or inventive as capitalism over the long term;
- Communist systems can result in better economic outcomes than exploitative capitalist systems—most Cuban citizens were better off after their communist revolution than they were under colonial capitalism; most Russian citizens were better off economically under the USSR than they are now under oligarchic capitalism;
- When it builds on a culture of communal values and production and when it empowers workers, communism can work reasonably well;
- External pressures can derail any inclination toward democracy in state-dominated systems;
- Central control can and frequently does devolve into bureaucracy and dictatorship, which tends to undermine the effectiveness of communist systems and result in human rights abuses.

When the USSR collapsed in 1990, most communist countries began a transition from communism to capitalism. The transition went very poorly in most cases. It proved much more difficult for communist countries that had little experience with markets to develop market-based economies than economists thought. Too little attention was paid to the need to develop all of the detailed legal and institutional structures and even the cultural characteristics that drive markets. Economists had evidently forgotten the lessons of history highlighted by Polanyi that the market system is complex and needs to be constructed carefully by the state. The biggest success story in the transition from a centrally planned economy to a market-based one was the case of China, which we turn to next.

8.6 THE CHINESE STATE DOMINATED ECONOMY

Under Mao Zedong, China's centrally planned economy emphasized rural industrialization, regional self-reliance, and decentralization. This differed dramatically from the centralized approach of the USSR. The Chinese government confiscated the lands of feudal lords and developed rural markets, giving farmers and workers more freedom and control over their work. This worked well initially, boosting productivity and rural incomes.

However, when the state tried to force farmers and workers into collectives, a more Soviet-style approach, the results were disastrous, with production declines, shortages, and extremely unhappy workers. In response, Mao implemented the "Hundred Flowers Campaign" and the "Great Leap Forward" to prompt creative thinking and solutions to the problems that China was experiencing. Efforts to develop the countryside utilizing traditional technology rather than cutting-edge methods did prompt the creation of numerous collective firms in rural China, which would later prove useful. However, the strategy was not effective in producing goods efficiently, and China again faced repeated shortages and crises. These crises led to the re-imposition of central planning, as China returned to a more traditional communist economy.

With Mao's death in 1976, the way was opened for a new approach led by Deng Xiaoping. Deng gradually incorporated market reforms into the centrally planned system. Communes were eliminated and rural farmers were granted property rights and the right to farm small private plots for their own benefit. The household once again became the main agricultural unit, and rural markets were created so farmers could sell their goods.

In a particularly adept policy, farmers and privatized small firms were required to sell a certain amount of produce to the state at a low price so that the state could preserve the central planning system. Any goods produced over the state quota could be sold in the newly created markets. This allowed enterprises to adapt to markets and market prices over time while preserving the stability of the economic system. Rather than experiencing a collapse as most communist countries did when markets were introduced, the gradual introduction of markets to China resulted in a huge economic boom.

Locally owned Town and Village Enterprises (TVEs), started under Mao's earlier efforts at rural industrialization, began to serve as a dynamic component of new markets. TVEs were owned by a village or town, were free from centralized control, and the manager was selected by local government officials. Profits from a TVE went to the community that owned it to pay wages, provide local public services, and generate funds for reinvestment. This gave TVEs an incentive to be successful, proving to be a source of entrepreneurship as the TVEs sought out niches in the newly created markets. By this point, China had moved away from a centrally planned, communist economy toward a Market Socialist Economy.

The creation of markets also involved the use of Special Economic Zones (SEZs) in China. SEZs were free trade zones within which firms could function in a market-based, capitalist manner while the rest of the economy was separate and protected. China attracted foreign investors to SEZs by offering low wages and taxes, few rules or regulations governing treatment of workers or the environment, a highly disciplined and skilled work force, and a devalued currency that made exporting from China extraordinarily profitable. In exchange for such attractive conditions, China mandated that foreign investors work with local partner firms and share their technology so that Chinese firms would gain experience with international manufacturing. Foreign firms were only too happy to comply with these conditions in order to gain access to the vast Chinese market.

Foreign investment poured in beginning in the 1980s. The SEZs coupled with the rural market reforms caused an astounding economic boom in China. From 1978–2016, China's per capita economic growth averaged 8.6% while most other countries were experiencing average growth rates of less than 2%! With this rate of growth, the Chinese economy has been doubling in size every 8.4 years. China is now the world's second largest economy and will likely pass the U.S. as the largest economy in 2029. China is now the world's largest exporting country, the largest manufacturer of automobiles, and the largest manufacturing country in general.

Although there is much economic independence of firms in China, the government still maintains a significant degree of control. The communist party preserves close ties to all large firms, and the Red Army even runs a lot of firms. The government determines the main direction of investment, and new ventures cannot take place without government approval. Some economists have actually referred to modern China as a form of state capitalism, given that the state is so closely involved in profit-making activities.

China is frequently criticized by other countries for its human rights violations and poor environmental record. Media and internet searches are still censored, and dissidents are regularly arrested and imprisoned. The student-led Tiananmen Square protests of 1989 were met with brutal repression, and between 200 and 1000 people were killed.[3] Since that crackdown, protests have been more muted. China is facing numerous ecological disasters thanks to its rapid growth without substantial environmental regulation. Its largest cities are choked with smog, and it also faces water and soil problems as well as habitat destruction and biodiversity loss.

It is not clear at this point if China will move in a more democratic direction or if it will continue to be led by a one-party, communist state. A 2014 Pew Research Global Attitudes survey indicated that Chinese citizens are more satisfied with the direction their country is heading than any other country in the world, with 87% of citizens satisfied (compared with 33% in the US). There appears to be no major pressures for change coming from within China.

China's success as a State Dominated Economy (SDE) has been matched to some degree by recent growth spurts in Russia and Brazil, who have also taken a state-directed approach to economic development. It is interesting that so many emerging markets are successfully adopting this approach. This seems to support the idea that utilizing an SDE approach in an underdeveloped country can be effective.

However, many other SDEs have been dismal failures when it comes to economic development. In countries where the state is kleptocratic—stealing resources for itself at the expense of the rest of society—or where the state bureaucracy is overly controlling and inefficient, SDEs tend to work very poorly. Dozens of countries have failed at utilizing a state-centered approach to development. There are actually more failures than success stories at this point, which you will study if you take a course on developing countries. Interestingly, it does not seem to matter if an abusive SDE adopts a capitalistic or a socialistic approach: Its stranglehold over the economy will stifle development either way. However, where SDEs work in the public interest and offer a more flexible, pragmatic approach, as is the case in China, the results can be quite positive.

8.7 CONCLUSION

This chapter has briefly sketched out the types of economic systems that we see in the modern world. Modern economic systems can be grouped into three broad categories: Market Dominated Economies, Social Market Economies, and State Dominated Economies. We have focused on successful, developed economies in this chapter as a guide to the possible recipes for economic prosperity.

The U.S. is the dominant MDE, generating high levels of income and wealth and spawning a noteworthy amount of innovation and entrepreneurship while struggling with inequality and poverty. The Nordic Model of an SME combines substantial government intervention with private sector development to achieve a similar level of income and innovation to the U.S. with fewer social problems. China's SDE has produced the most rapid rate of growth in the world for 40 years, a remarkable, sustained success story marred by human rights abuses and significant environmental problems.

In the modern economic systems we see reflections of the ideas of the great economists that we studied earlier. In a nod to Adam Smith, all modern economies use market capitalism substantially. Fueled by competition, markets produce the products that consumers want while keeping prices low and fostering innovations. In a nod to Karl Marx, all economic systems work to safeguard the rights and safety of laborers and use the state to make peoples' lives better than the market would on its own. Two countries, Cuba and North Korea, still reject capitalism and espouse a communist philosophy. Reflecting Veblen's ideas, modern economies work to promote the productive side of markets, striving to develop new, productive industries via public-private partnerships. But, responding to Hayek's cautions, most economic systems are wary of having too much state interference in the economy. Ultimately, all modern economic systems reflect the ideas of John Maynard Keynes, having developed mixed economic systems that rely on market capitalism for some economic decisions while using the state for others. What is interesting is the variation one finds in modern economic systems, with MDEs leaning more towards Smith, SDEs leaning more towards Marx, and SMEs in the middle.

QUESTIONS FOR REVIEW

1. Explain the key differences between Market Dominated Economies, Social Market Economies and State Dominated Economies. Use specific examples to support your answer.
2. What are the key elements of the U.S. MDE? What factors do you think are essential contributors to U.S. economic success? What are the major problems with the U.S. MDE?
3. What are the key elements of the Nordic SME? What factors do you think are essential contributors to its economic success? What problems do you see with the SME approach?
4. How do socialism and communism differ from capitalism?
5. What are the strengths and weaknesses of a market capitalist approach (U.S.), a guided market approach (Nordic Model), and a central planning approach (USSR) to economic development?
6. The most successful countries in the last 50 years have used the government extensively in economic development efforts. However, many developing countries in sub-Saharan Africa, Latin America, and Southeast Asia have adopted similar approaches with little success.

Why might a government-centered approach to development have such an uneven track record?

7. What are the key ingredients in China's economic success? Why was China's transition from a centrally planned system to a market-oriented system more successful than the transition in Russia?

8. Innovation is a key ingredient in economic success over time. What are the lessons regarding innovation that emerge from the experiences of the countries described in this chapter?

9. Write an essay in which you compare and contrast the U.S. economic system with the Nordic Model. In your essay, take up the following issues: (a) What role does government play in each economy? (b) How does each economy reflect the ideas of Adam Smith, Karl Marx, Thorstein Veblen, John Maynard Keynes, and Friedrich Hayek? (c) What are the strengths and weaknesses of each economic system?

10. What role does culture seem to play in structuring economic systems? Explain using specific examples.

11. Would it be possible to implement a Social Market Economy in the United States? Why or why not?

NOTES

1. Mukherjee, Satyam, Daniel Romero, Benjamin F. Jones and Brian Uzzi, "The Nearly Universal Link Between the Age of Past Knowledge and Tomorrow's Breakthroughs in Science and Technology," *Science Advances*, 3, 4 (19 Apr 2017).

2. Note that the co-determination system has been weakened in recent years in the face of global competition. It will be interesting to see how much of this system is maintained in the future. Given that it is credited with Germany's much-vaunted labor skill and productivity, it is difficult to imagine the system going away altogether.

3. Official Chinese Government estimates range from 200–300 while journalists put the number of deaths between 300–1000.

Glossary of key terms and concepts

Austerity: a government policy to reduce or eliminate social programs like food stamps, unemployment insurance, and education, in order to balance the government budget.

Business cycle: the pattern of booms and busts created by economic fluctuations in market capitalist economies.

Capital goods: the machinery, equipment, buildings, and productive resources (other than labor) used to produce goods and services.

Capitalism: an economic system in which the capital goods and other productive resources (land, natural resources) are privately owned and are bought and sold in markets based on the pursuit of profits.

***Ceteris paribus* assumption:** all other relevant factors do not change.

Choice: when consumers, producers, and governments select from among the limited options that are available to them due to scarcity.

Class: a group of people that has a specific relationship with the production process (e.g., capitalists, workers, slaves, lords).

Collective bargaining: when workers bargain as a group (union) with employers instead of each worker bargaining separately with an employer.

Communism: an economic system in which the government controls society's productive resources and makes the major economic decisions.

Communist economic system: an economic system in which the means of production and distribution are publicly owned and each person works according to their abilities and is paid according to their needs (e.g., the U.S.S.R., Cuba).

Conspicuous consumption: the practice of consumers purchasing and using goods for the purposes of displaying their status and importance to others.

Consumer goods: goods that are purchased and used by consumers, but that do not contribute to future productivity.

Creative destruction: the process by which businesses are forced to invent constantly to stay one step ahead of the competition, and where creative, new industries inevitably destroy and replace older ones.

Democratic socialism: an economic system in which the most important resources of society are controlled democratically by all citizens, including workers who usually have little say in how market capitalist economies are run.

Dialectics: a method of analysis focusing on contradictions and the struggle of opposing forces.

Double movement: Polanyi's term for the push for the development of markets by businesses (first mercantilists and then capitalists) which was met by a counter movement by workers and communities to regulate markets.

Economic model: a theoretical, simplified construct designed to focus on a key set of economic relationships.

Efficiency: in mainstream economics, a situation in which all resources are employed as productively as possible.

Government: provides the institutions that develop and implement policies for the state.

Historical materialism: Marx's approach to the study of economics, which focuses on the class conflicts and technological changes that provoke changes in the material conditions of society over time.

Imperialism: when one country gains control of another country or territory.

Infant industry promotion strategy: a country protects and subsidizes a new industry until it can be globally competitive.

Institutional economics: the study of the institutions that shape an economy, how the economy and those institutions evolve, and how human beings are shaped by culture and institutions and seek status and power within those structures.

Institutions: the organizations, social structures, rules, and habits that structure human interactions and the economy.

Law of increasing opportunity cost: if resources are specialized and if all resources are being used efficiently, then as more and more of one good is produced, the opportunity cost of producing each additional unit of that good will increase.

Macroeconomic problems created by wage and price deflation: declines in wages undermine aggregate demand and declines in prices undermine business profitability, both of which harm the economy in particular ways.

Macroeconomics: the study of the aggregate forces that shape national economies.

Mainstream economics (ME): the study of how society manages its scarce resources to satisfy individuals' unlimited wants.

Marginal Productivity Theory of Distribution: the neoclassical theory that people are paid exactly what they are worth based on their marginal productivity under a competitive, capitalist economic system. This theory assumes that there are no power imbalances, so no exploitative relationships exist.

Market Dominated Economies (MDEs): economic systems in which the primary economic decisions are made by private actors (businesses, individuals) in the market. Government and social values play a secondary role.

Markets Always Clear: The neoclassical theory that supply always equals demand in all markets, so the invisible hand of the market always allocates resources efficiently.

Mixed market capitalism: an economic system in which private sector firms and individuals produce goods and services for markets for profits, and a public sector established by the government regulates those markets and provides public goods such as schools, roads, airports, health care, and other goods and services that are usually provided inadequately by private markets.

Monopoly power: the ability of large firms to control prices.

Multiplier process: A respending process whereby a dollar in spending becomes income for someone else, which they then spend, which becomes additional income, and so on, so that a dollar of spending is respent multiple times.

Necessary product: the resources necessary for a community's survival, including food, shelter, and the replacement of tools and materials used up in production.

Neoclassical economics: the study of how rational actors in competitive markets determine incomes and the prices and quantities of goods and services through the interaction of supply and demand.

Opportunity cost: what is given up when a choice is made to allocate resources in a particular way.

Pecuniary emulation: when people from the lower classes imitate the culture, habits, and spending of the upper classes to achieve status for themselves.

Pluralistic economics: a social science whose practitioners, from a variety of distinct schools of thought, study economies, how they grow and change, and the how they produce and distribute the goods societies need and want.

Production possibilities curve (PPC):   a model that shows all combinations of 2 goods that can be produced, holding the amount of resources and the level of technology fixed.

Progressive political economics (PPE):   the study of social provisioning—the economic processes that provide the goods and services required by society to meet the needs of its members.

Property rights: when a productive resource, such as land or a slave, belongs to a particular person or group instead of to society as a whole.

Radical political economics (RPE):   the study of power relations in society, especially conflicts over the allocation of a society's resources by various social classes (e.g., capitalists and workers), and how those conflicts cause society to evolve.

Says Law: supply creates its own demand, and savings is always equal to investment.

Scarcity: when a society's seemingly unlimited desire for goods and services exceeds the resources available to produce and provide those goods and services.

Social Market Economies (SMEs):   economic systems in which social values take a leading role in directing the economy, usually through the actions of a government which manages the economy in accordance with social values.

Socialist economic system: an economic system in which the means of production and distribution are either owned or regulated by society.

Specialization of labor: particular tasks are performed by specific individuals, rather than everyone performing all tasks.

Specialization of resources: when some resources cannot be easily adapted from one use to another.

Stabilization policy: increasing government spending, reducing taxes, and reducing interest rates in recessions, while doing the opposite when the economy is growing too quickly.

Stagflation: stagnation and inflation at the same time.

State Dominated Economies (SDEs): economic systems in which the government is the main economic actor in most major industries or economic decisions, owning or controlling most of the economy.

Status-seeking: the human propensity to try to achieve the highest social status possible, as defined by the particular culture of the community.

Sticky wages and prices: in a recession, wages and prices do not fall fast enough to encourage businesses to hire more workers and consumers to buy more goods.

Surplus product: the amount that is produced over and above what is needed for the community's survival (the necessary product).

Surplus value: the amount of value produced by workers over and above the cost of their wages (including benefits).

Technology: the tools, skills, and scientific knowledge that society develops in the use of resources to produce goods and services.

Traditional economy: an economy in which resources are allocated based on communal patterns of reciprocity and redistribution, and in which tasks are allocated and knowledge and skills preserved through established social relationships.

Unregulated market capitalism: an economic system in which the main productive resources of society—the labor, land, machinery, equipment, and natural resources—are owned by private individuals, who use those resources to produce goods and services that are bought and sold in markets for profits.

Vested interests: the group dominating society whose goal is usually to preserve the status quo that it benefits from.

Volatility of investment: the Keynesian theory that business purchases of capital goods (investment) depend primarily on expected future profits, which is driven largely by expected sales, and expectations can vary dramatically.

Index